• HALSGROVE DISCOVER SERIES ➤

CORNWALL'S CHINA CLAY COUNTRY

Settling tank. Adrian Brown

• HALSGROVE DISCOVER SERIES ➤

CORNWALL'S CHINA CLAY COUNTRY

EXPLORING THE LAND OF THE WHITE PYRAMID

Roger Fogg

Colour photographs by Adrian Brown

HALSGROVE

First published in Great Britain in 2011

Copyright © Roger Fogg & Adrian Brown 2011

All rights reserved. No part of this publication may be reproduced, stored in a retrieval system, or transmitted in any form or by any means without the prior permission of the copyright holder.

British Library Cataloguing-in-Publication Data
A CIP record for this title is available from the British Library

ISBN 978 0 85704 103 6

HALSGROVE
Halsgrove House,
Ryelands Business Park,
Bagley Road, Wellington, Somerset TA21 9PZ
Tel: 01823 653777   Fax: 01823 216796
email: sales@halsgrove.com

Part of the Halsgrove group of companies
Information on all Halsgrove titles is available at: www.halsgrove.com

Printed in China by Everbest Printing Co Ltd

Opposite: *Blackpool Pit.* Adrian Brown

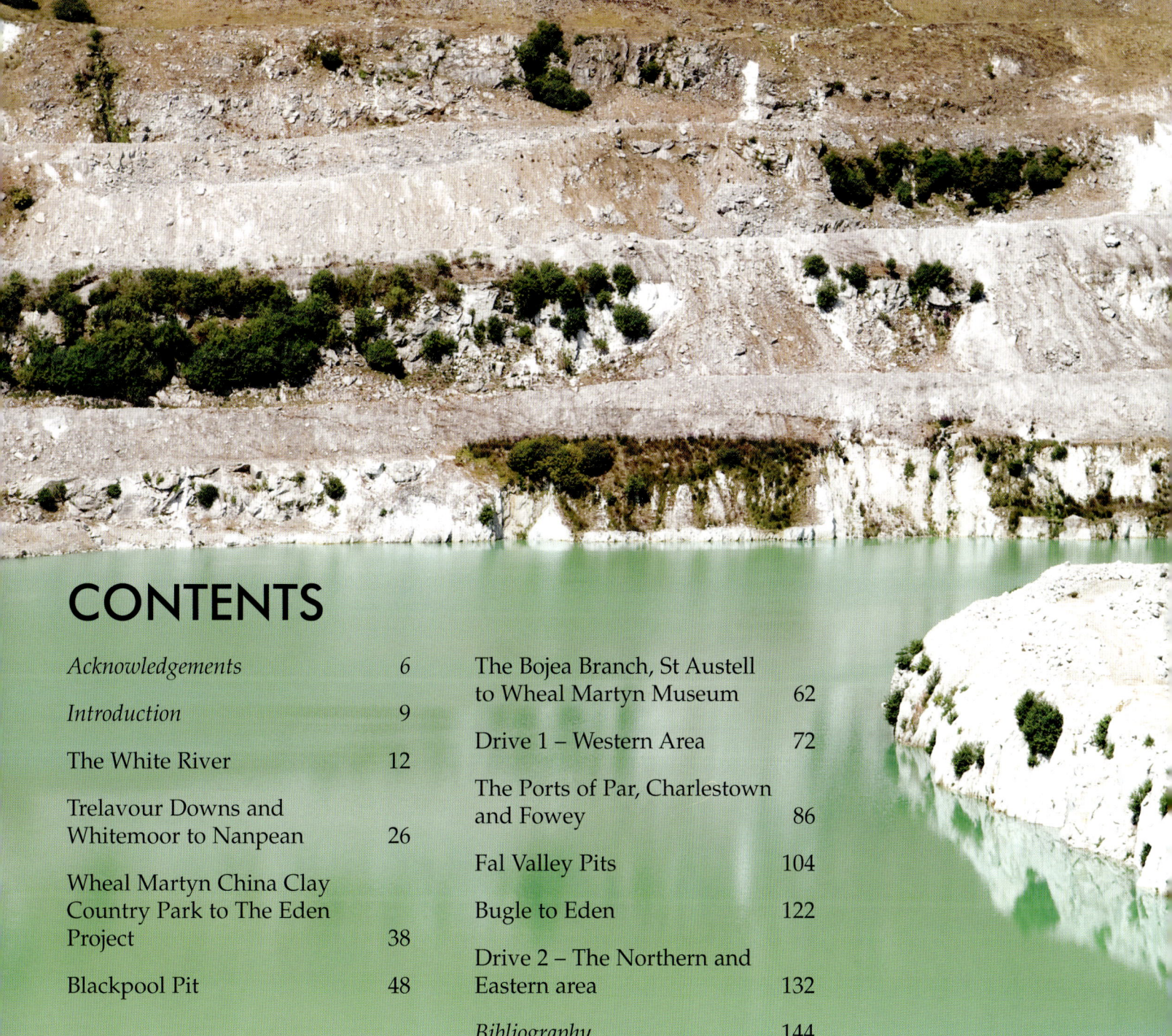

CONTENTS

Acknowledgements	6
Introduction	9
The White River	12
Trelavour Downs and Whitemoor to Nanpean	26
Wheal Martyn China Clay Country Park to The Eden Project	38
Blackpool Pit	48
The Bojea Branch, St Austell to Wheal Martyn Museum	62
Drive 1 – Western Area	72
The Ports of Par, Charlestown and Fowey	86
Fal Valley Pits	104
Bugle to Eden	122
Drive 2 – The Northern and Eastern area	132
Bibliography	144

ACKNOWLEDGEMENTS

THIS BOOK COULD NOT have been created without the help and advice given by members of the China Clay History Society. They have a wealth of knowledge and resources and have shared it generously. Derek Giles, Richard Puttick and Ivor Bowditch have given their time and energy to offer advice and to source photographs from the extensive archive over which they preside. Ivor Bowditch in particular spent a lot of time putting the facts straight. Sometimes when writing a book like this it is easy to repeat tales and stories that have little basis in truth. As far as possible we have tried to go to original sources and Ivor, who is one of the most knowledgeable people on the history and present day workings of the china clay industry, guided us in the right direction. The CHSS is based at Wheal Martyn Museum and further information on this most excellent society is available from there.

We must also thank Sam Edyvean for allowing us to make use of his collection of postcards, photographs and ephemera that go to build a picture of the area, he could not have been more helpful. We have talked to many people and heard lots of anecdotes, some of which are included within these pages. There are friends who have walked the routes and checked them out for mistakes; similarly there are those who have helped with proof reading and offered general help and support. So thanks to Sam Edyvean, Tatum, Teo and Koben Triggs, John Stephens, Nikolai and Lukas Holse, Carl Triggs, Imerys and Goonvean China Clay Companies, Martin Milton, Sarah Franks, Henry Tabb, Helen Campbell, Andrew Northam, Ian Thompson Tom Seward and Andrew Fogg. Apologies to those we have missed.

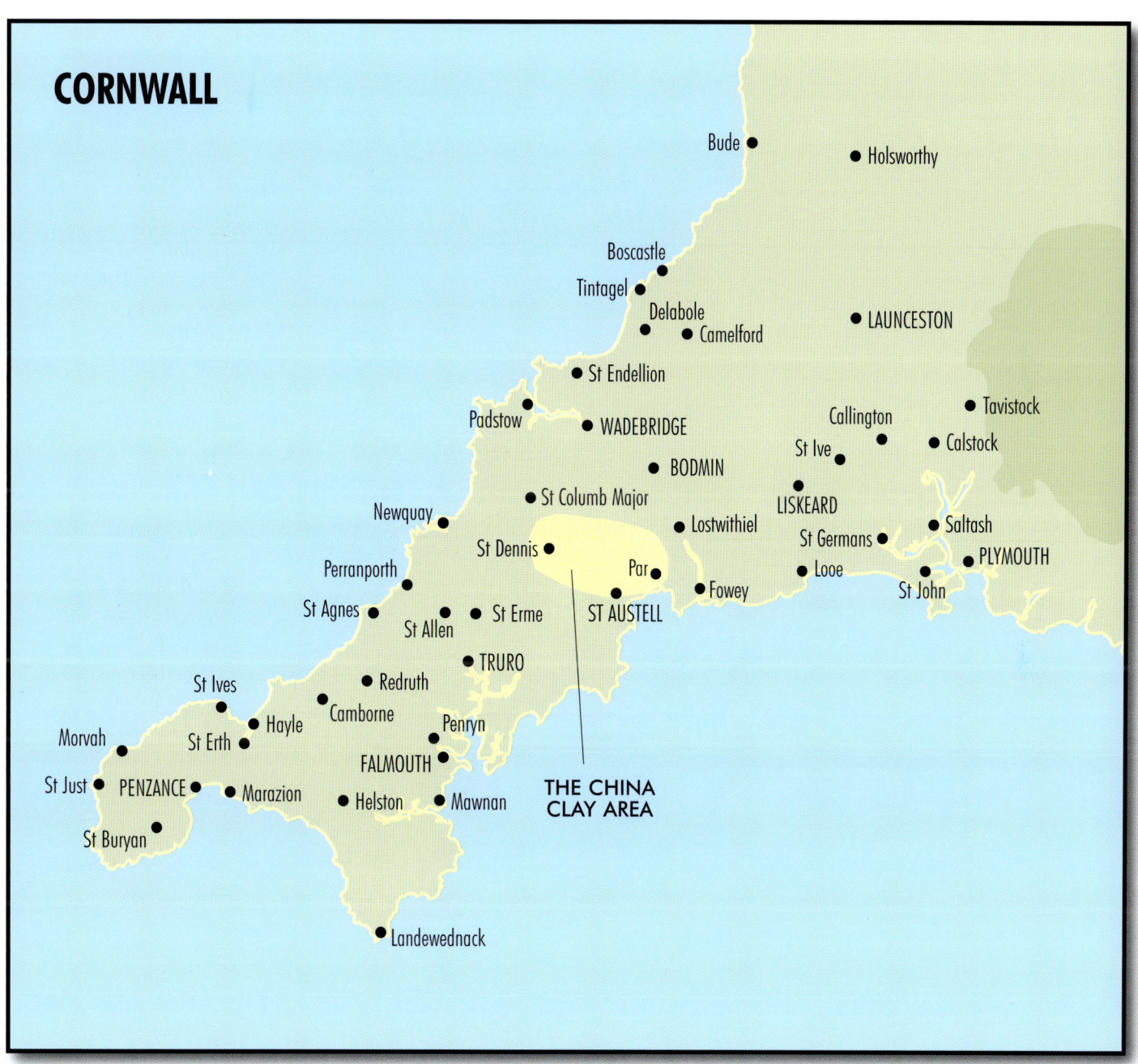

Claycountry landscape at Nanpean. Adrian Brown

INTRODUCTION

THE GRANITE UPLANDS around St Austell have been at the centre of the china clay industry for more than two hundred years yet they remain almost unknown to outsiders. Visitors speeding down the Goss Moor on their way to the beaches and holiday resorts further to the west of the County may be aware of the strange silhouettes and hills of the area, but their thoughts are on the sands and the seaside delights that await them. Retirees may pause on their coastal walks to gaze inland; holidaymakers flying into Newquay may wonder briefly what the strangely coloured lakes below might be. Tourists on their way to the Eden Project in coaches may get a commentary on the remarkable landscape but rarely do they stop and investigate further. Even those who live in other parts of Cornwall have only a vague idea of what goes on in the mines and refineries, the dryers and the ports.

China clay, kaolin, was formed by the gradual decomposition over millions of years of the granite rocks in the area. By far the biggest buyer of the clay that is produced is the paper industry, taking around 80% of production, but china clay is also used in ceramics, medicine, as a food additive, in toothpaste, light bulbs and cosmetics. It is the main component in porcelain and goes into the manufacture of paint, rubber and adhesives.

The main clay mining area covers only around 25 square miles to the north of St Austell, yet it has produced a way of life, a culture and a language form that is quite unique. The remains of past times here is very much in evidence in the shape of the waste tips or burrows as they are known locally; there are disused buildings, picturesque ruins and abandoned pits, yet alongside these are modern workings, deep quarries and industry on a vast scale. Tin mines and miners have long been celebrated in word and picture, although the Cornish miner is seen as someone from the distant past with little connection to the twenty-first century. Nevertheless, despite the clay industry being in decline, there are still many men and women who make their living by digging minerals out of the ground in Cornwall. They are following a way of life that has gone on for generations, and which continues to do so whilst there are adequate reserves of clay in the ground, and it is economical to keep production going. In many ways the China Clay area is one of the last strongholds of the indigenous Cornish people; they have always lived here because unlike the tin miners there was never a need to go elsewhere: whilst the clay lasted so did the workers.

This book seeks to explore the St Austell china clay area and to help visitors interpret what they see, and locals to remember how things were. Purposely, it also serves to highlight what continues to be a very important industry in Cornwall. Through a series of walks and drives around the district the authors have tried to convey not just the history of the area but also the sense that there is rather more to this place than simply a semi-derelict industrial wasteland. Following the routes of clay trails that have been established around the disused mines there are point-by-point explanations of what can be observed by walkers, cyclists and in a couple of cases drivers and their passengers. Period photographs illustrate bygone methods of winning the clay, the buildings that were once so typical of the industry and the people that did the work. The recent colour photographs reinforce impressions of a modern landscape that is quite unique to this part of Cornwall. Please bear in mind that the walks were correct at the time of writing. However because some of the paths are permissive and also because of the dynamic nature of the mining activities, occasionally there could be some minor variations to the routes as they are written. Take care while walking, don appropriate clothing and footwear, and carrying the relevant OS map for the area is highly recommended if not essential.

It is always the far west of the County or the honeypots on the coast and moors that have traditionally inspired artists, writers and poets. It seems a great pity that more time has not been devoted to this area. There are opportunities here to see lost valleys, massive machines at work, stunning views, historic buildings and traditional architecture. Perhaps after reading this book there will be those who will look at the pits and tips, the working quarries and ports, the railways, the factories and the houses, and above all the people who live here, in a different light. There are many aspects of the area that we have barely touched upon in this book but we hope that you will be inspired and intrigued by what has been included. Enjoy the area while you can, it may not last much longer!

INTRODUCTION

China Clay Country. Adrian Brown

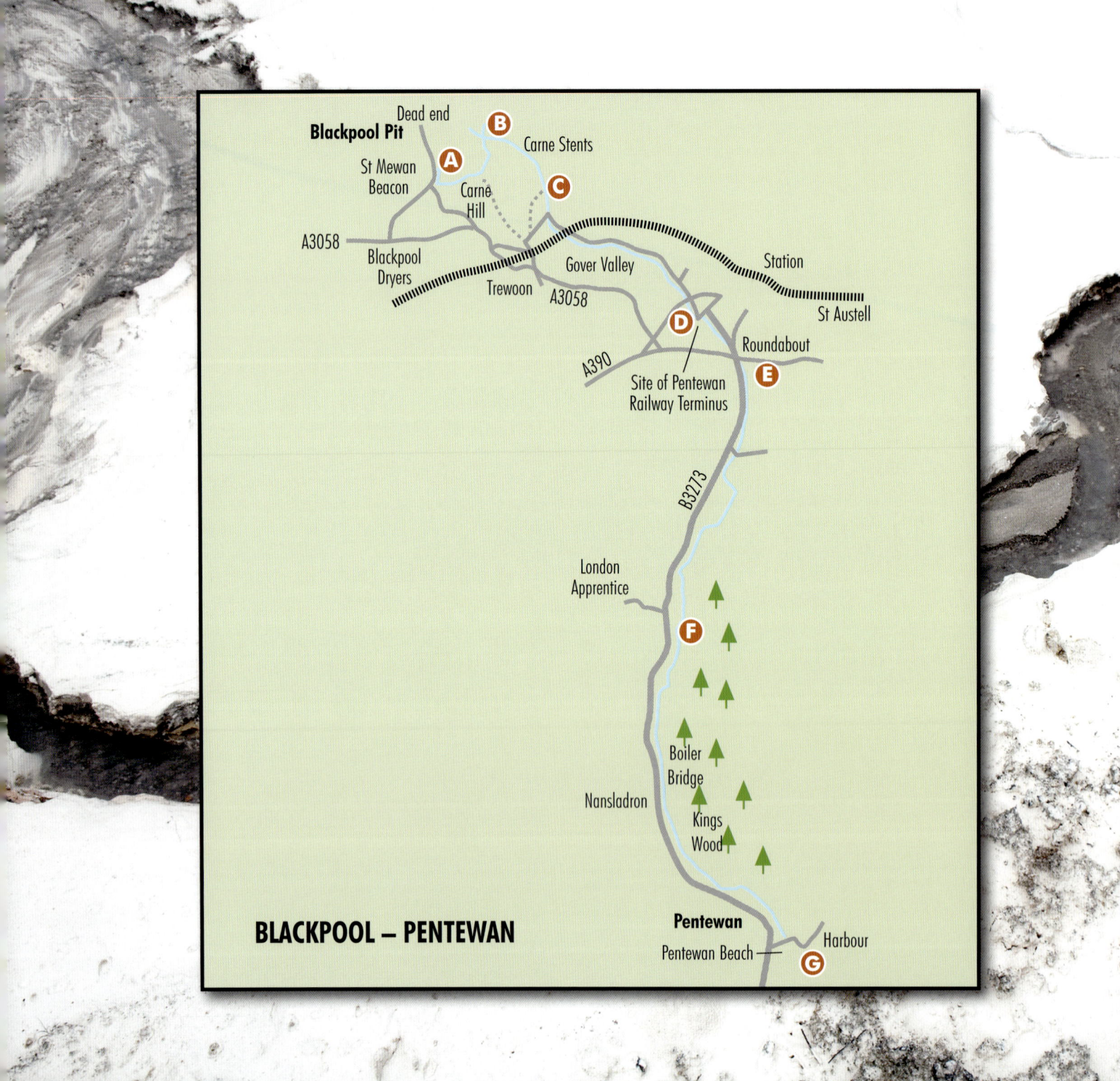

THE WHITE RIVER

THE RIVER THAT RUNS from Hensbarrow through St Austell and down the Pentewan Valley to the sea is called The White River. Although its proper name is The Winnick it is almost universally known by that name on account of the colour of the clay residue that it carried and which turned it completely white. Any small clear tributaries that may have entered from side valleys stood no chance against the all pervasive colouration of the main watercourse. The river contributed as much to the unique landscape of the area as any of the towering sand burrows or deep pits that dominate the skyline. This walk is intended to follow the present day White River from its source in the hills to its entry into the sea. Although the lower part of the route from St Austell down to Pentewan is well documented, the upper reaches of the river are less well known. The beginnings of the walk have to be just that, there are only footpaths; cycles cannot use these old tracks, so the bicycle rider and pram pusher really has to start part way down! From beginning to end it is around 6 miles long, and like many of the trails this one can easily be divided into separate parts such that some may wish to retrace their footsteps after a while. St Austell and Pentewan have toilets, cafes and car parks.

This aerial shot of Pentewan Beach in the early sixties graphically illustrates the extent of the pollution carried down from the china clay mines by the White River. The beach owes more to the hills around St Austell than to sand naturally washed in from the sea.

C Edyvean

The White River, like so many rivers, can claim to have more than one source. The true locations of the springs that combine to form the upper waters probably lie buried deep beneath hundreds of thousands of tons of waste. Two main valleys and their streams join together in St Austell to become the main course. The Trenance Valley brings its water from high up beyond the China Clay Museum, whilst the Gover Valley, the one with which we are concerned, divides off and follows a different route to Burngullow Common above the village of Trewoon. When the expansion of Littlejohns, Wheal Martyn Pit and their associated works occurred in the 1970s and 80s, the large sand burrows which can be seen around 'The New Road' were created by infilling an area of fields, moorland and marshy ground. There was a tremendous amount of spoil to be dumped and a new highway that was constructed to replace the older network of roads which had been destroyed provided a natural boundary. The built up road embankment crossing the top of the valley defined the limits of the area allocated for tipping. A long concrete tunnel

Carne Stents in the Gover Valley. Adrian Brown

was built enclosing the course of the small stream in the original valley bottom which continued beneath the embankment, exiting on the lower side.

On the higher side the tip was begun. At first the natural valley was below the level of the road. Slowly the tip encroached, the concrete tunnel was buried, and along with it disappeared the field systems, mature trees, river bank habitats and any remains of what had gone before. Inexorably the tip grew higher and higher. What was once a road which traversed the head of a valley, now defined the base of a tip many hundreds of metres high. But despite the fact that the real source of the river is lost forever, we can still enjoy what remains, and explore this little known part of the district.

(A) The start of the walk is above the Village of Trewoon on the main A3058 Newquay road out of St Austell, and can be reached by a bus which goes there from St Austell. On the way out of Trewoon, just before the pub, there is a road that goes off to the right called Carne Hill. Go up past the Kingdom Hall of Jehovah Witnesses and at the T-junction, close to St Mewan Beacon, there is a sign for a footpath. If there is a need to park a car then a layby a bit further on can be used. At this stage it needs to be made clear that we shall follow public rights of way. Locals may well know of other tracks, indeed right opposite the layby marked by two rocks is the start of one such well used path, but this is private land!

So follow the Public Footpath sign by the little grassy triangle at the top of Carne Hill and go through the avenue of Leylandi trees. Although this is a private drive, the path goes round the back of the buildings to the left and from there into a lane. Follow the lane down through and on a corner go through a gate into a field on the left, despite the fact that the lane itself bears right and continues between tree lined hedges in the general direction of Trewoon. Once in the field, keep the hedge on the left. The very distinct boundary between the agricultural and clay producing land becomes very apparent with grazing cattle and crops in the fields contrasting with the wilder moorland, overgrown tips and modern clay workings. This is one of the last high places where the course of the river can be seen and its path imagined from source to sea, though blocked from view by the trees and valleys. Hidden away, just a few fields distant is Carne Stents, another one of those dark lonely pools that is hardly ever visited and which has developed a habitat all of its own. In spring the banks are covered with a myriad of tiny frogs, newly mobile and seeking to escape the waters and find freedom in the surrounding undergrowth. Crows and seagulls soar up here, but the wind blows and the rain sweeps in from the sea at all times of year.

The Pentewan railway emerged from the woods and passed the ponds which had been built in a vain attempt to sluice the harbour free of sand. The buildings associated with the docks can be seen here as can the beach in whose creation the White River played such a significant part.
C Edyvean

CORNWALL'S CHINA CLAY COUNTRY

The 15th century pack horse bridge which crosses the St Austell River is now closed to traffic but the whiteness of the river from the clay pollution can be made out in this 1950s postcard.

C Edyvean

Turn a corner and the path comes to a stile in the hedge where immediately a new and different countryside emerges. Almost at once the land starts to fall away quite steeply. This is mostly disturbed ground, a place where rubble was tipped many years ago, a site that would once have seen all kinds of industrial activities but which was abandoned to nature some time after the Second World War. The muddy and sometimes difficult track descends through rhododendron woods, gorse, bluebells, brambles, willow, ash and stunted oaks. At a small crossroads the path goes straight across; turn left and you end up by Carne Stents Pool. There is a steep and neglected set of steps that have to be negotiated carefully; equally awkward is the wooden bridge which crosses the small stream that is the tributary of the White River. **(B)** From now on the sight and sound of this small stream will always be close, the water getting deeper and wider as it nears St Austell and eventually the sea. Turn right and its all downhill to another small clay work which is part of Carne Stents.

On the left are high stone walls and it is worth pausing just to look at the size of the stones that are built into it at a great height and imagine what it would have been like to manhandle them up there in the days before mechanical help was readily available. The

In this old print the Winnick, later called the White River, flows under the original West Bridge on the Truro Road out of St Austell. In the eighteenth century the river was clear enough to fish in.

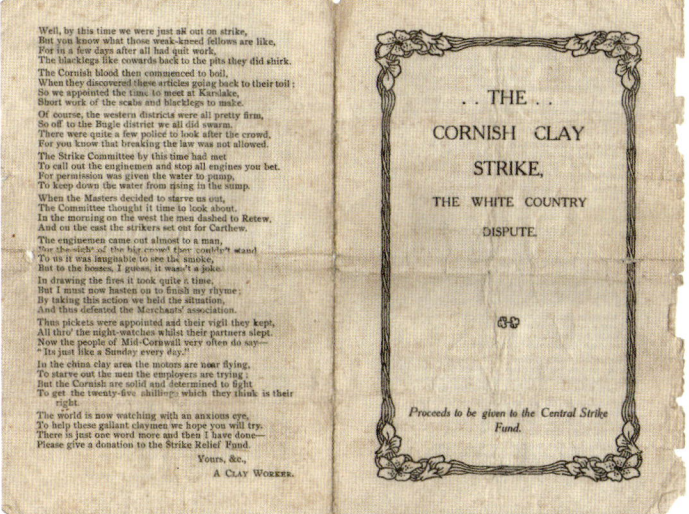
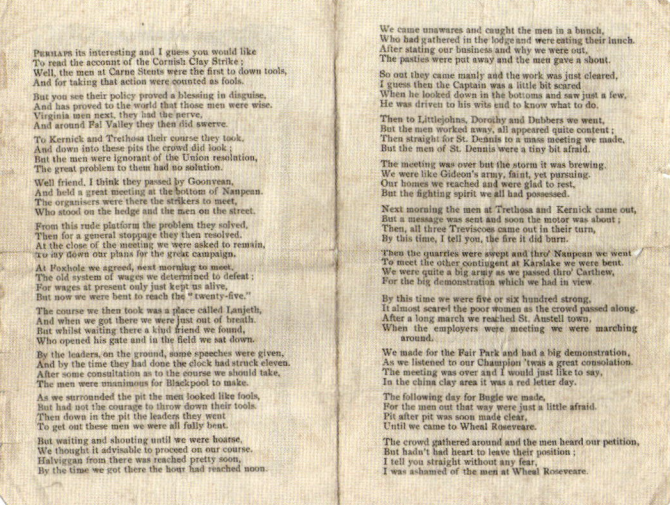

brick arch and flues that can still be seen easily identify this building as a clay dry. Underneath are the brick piles that supported the drying floors as the hot air and smoke passed beneath and exited up the chimney at the other end. Just a bit further on are the remains of some moss-covered mica drags and sluices, they provide plain evidence that, once the clay-stained water was used and as much clay as possible had been recovered, it was directed straight into the river and allowed to run out to sea. The valley off to the left is picturesque but is a dead end and terminates in a barbed wire fence. The path continues to descend following the river as it tumbles through a rocky defile. Notice the great rounded boulders and think how they got here! There are still places where the road has been shored up to stop it falling into the stream; this has been a problem for as long as the road has existed, maintenance would have been paramount in order to get the raw materials out and supplies to keep the mine working in. Carne Stents achieved some form of notoriety in the distant past as the place where the 1913 Clay Strike first saw the miners down tools. From here the dispute spread to other works and villages, its course can be charted in the poem included in this book. A television programme called 'Stockers Copper' was made about the strike some years ago. Medland Stocker owned the mine and was instrumental in bringing in a group of policeman from South Wales and Bristol to break the strike, a task in which he eventually succeeded

Soon the track widens, more cottages and mine workings appear, there are kennels in a former dryer, and further on down the valley additional houses and converted buildings

The clay strike of 1913 affected most of the pits in the area. Although the strike was eventually broken, for a while it united the clay miners throughout mid Cornwall. This pamphlet was written and sold to support the strikers' cause.

C Edyvean

Gover Mill just out of St Austell used an overshot water wheel but it dealt with tin rather than clay. The White River passes beside the road which leads to the terminus of the Pentewan Railway just beyond the trees. Nothing now remains of these buildings.

C Edyvean

reveal themselves. From this point on cycling is easy and permissible. In a short while the sandy track turns to tarmac and is joined on the right by a very steep road known as Stoney Hill that leads up to the village of Trewoon. **(C)** A little way before this there is a track signed 'Path to Trewoon' that provides a muddier but safer alternative to the Stoney Hill short cut, and which comes out at the top of the hill there. This may be a good place to return to the start for those who wish to do so, and by simply walking up the hill and turning right at the top into the track by the bungalows the route goes back to St Mewan Beacon again.

On the left, behind the newly recommissioned works and attendant chimney is a sand burrow known locally as Teddy Bear. The origins of this nickname are obscure, one suggestion that so far has that not been explored and was advanced some years ago refers to the fact that the hill is covered in gorse or fuzzy bushes, so the little piece of doggerel that goes 'fuzzy wuzzy was a bear' may provide the key to the riddle. Prove that theory wrong if you can...' ...More likely is that the official name 'Trembear' Clay Works has been corrupted in local use.

Passing beneath Brunel's railway viaduct with the stream happily babbling away beside the road, the fingers of urbanisation have reached up the valley and a housing estate now

Gover Valley in 1920 showing a wagon coming up the valley with a load of coal for the kilns at Carne Stents. The waggoner is believed to be named Borlaze, the boy is George Growden. The state of the roads indicates how the wooden cartwheels cut up the surface.

CCHS

THE WHITE RIVER

Gover Kiln. The remains of these buildings below Carne Stents can be seen hidden on the left of the track across the river as it descends the valley.

CCHS

dominates the scenery. Japanese Knotweed has had a big impact on the little meadows here and spraying has taken place in an effort to eradicate this invasive plant. Still there are ghosts of former industrial buildings and on a corner are the remains of Gover Mill, which was associated with the extraction of iron and tin and was powered by water from the stream.

Now the road gets busy, and there are houses all around. The river disappears from view for a while but is never far away. On the right are some warehouse style retail outlets, of no particular interest, but they are built on the site of Hill & Philips Garage. This was where Captain Percival Philips kept his Avro 504K aircraft with which he used to travel all around the country giving joy rides to fare-paying passengers. There is clearly no airfield at this site, so alternative arrangements were made. The planes of the St Austell Aviation Company were serviced and managed from this garage, and then with the wings detached and taken separately, they were pulled behind a car up the hill to Rocky Park near St Mewan School where they were re assembled ready for take off. Many thousands of people had their fist experience of flying with Captain Philips at the controls, although unfortunately he was killed when he crashed his aircraft in February 1938 near St Neots in Cambridgeshire.

The Avro 504K belonging to The Cornwall Aviation Company with Captain Phillips at the controls. This aircraft was kept at the garage in the Gover Valley and towed up Truro Road behind a car to the grass airstrip at Rocky Park near St Mewan.

C Edyvean

CORNWALL'S CHINA CLAY COUNTRY

This Victorian postcard shows the steep West Hill leading down to the terminus of the Pentewan Railway in St Austell, not easy with a fully laden wagon! This is now the site of the West End Fish and Chip Shop.

C Edyvean

Continue over the crossroads by the traffic lights, on the left is the only high-rise tower block in Cornwall, and soon there is a pub and next to it a small supermarket. This is the site of the terminus of the Pentewan Railway at West Hill and marks the beginning of the second part of the White River's journey from source to sea. A good place to park, go up to the town or find a pub for refreshments. The White River is still there, the old pack horse bridge is on the other side of the Western Inn, although it is now for pedestrian use only.

(D) The Pentewan Railway is well documented and there are several publications available which go into detail about its history and final demise. Briefly it was built to take China Clay from St Austell down to the harbour at Pentewan for onward shipment. At first it was horse drawn only although because of the gentle gradient the unhitched wagons could be rolled for some distance just using gravity before they needed an extra pull. Apparently a good shove on the loaded wagons would make them reach such a speed that a man on a galloping horse would have trouble keeping up! The journey back from the sea was accomplished using horses the whole way. The wagons were not always empty, they often had wood, coal and other materials for the St Austell mines brought in

THE WHITE RIVER

The St Austell terminus of the Pentewan Railway in 1910. The three horse wagons that had come down Gover Valley loaded with clay for the railway were refilled with timber and coal to resupply the mines on the way back.
CCHS

The Entrance to Pentewan was constantly under threat from the enormous quantities of sand which was washed down the White River from the mines. Eventually it became too much to clear and the harbour completely silted up and remains so to this day.
C Edyvean

The railway engine 'Canopus' at the end of a railway outing in Pentewan. For the whole of its existence this little engine was only ever run by a father and son crew.
CCHS

CORNWALL'S CHINA CLAY COUNTRY

Though not on the route of this walk, Adrian Brown's atmospheric photograph of overgrown clay dries evokes memories of a once vibrant industry now almost completely lost to time and decay.

Adrian Brown

by the sailing ships. It was a slow and strenuous journey for the animals and their drivers; as a result in the 1870s steam locomotives were introduced and the track was reduced to a narrower gauge.

Although there were proposals to take the railway much further into the clay producing areas, outline plans to take the tracks up the Gover and Trenance valleys never came to fruition. Hence all traffic started and finished at this terminus. Loaded horse-drawn clay wagons had to make their way down steep hills and along poor roads to transfer their loads on to the railway trucks at West Hill. At Pentewan there was another movement of the raw materials into the holds of ships, a costly exercise in terms of manpower. By contrast main line trains were running deep into the valleys where loads were put straight on to the trucks from the clay stores known as 'linhays' close to the mines themselves, then taken directly away with very little fuss or extra work. The little railway played a big part in the life and fortunes of the Pentewan Valley, but the instability of the track bed through flooding, and the silting up of the harbour often disrupted regular service. Even so a lot of clay was shifted in the years between 1873 and the start of the First World War. In 1918 the Government requisitioned the engines, rolling stock and rails for the war effort; although it is said that in fact they were never used again. And so this marked the end of the Pentewan railway for ever.

The site now occupied by the supermarket and its car park were the loading areas, full of sidings, ramps, stables, maintenance sheds and all the general paraphernalia associated with a busy industrial railhead. Little now remains, although one or two older buildings survive, including one which has a cast iron plate attached to it by The Old Cornwall Society explaining its origins. This small building stands next to the Supermarket on the track of the old railway. The trail here can be followed down a rather muddy and unattractive path along the back of the houses in Moorland Road. It exits on to the main St Austell by pass at the Mevagissey Roundabout. Care has to be taken when crossing here; the traffic can sometimes be a little confusing!

(E) Take the Mevagissey road, the B3273, past Macdonalds, B & Q and the few bungalows and out into the country. The shopping complex on the right was once the home of John Williams & Co, an offshoot of the clay industry which employed a small army of carpenters who were involved in the manufacture of windows, doors and the like, including those for the Cornish Unit houses being produced by the company elsewhere. Next door to that were the ECLP laboratories which researched and tested the minerals that were being produced. Macdonalds and the hotel next to it are standing on the site of the former Cattle Market. The nearest place for local farmers to meet and sell their animals is now in Truro, perhaps reflecting the changing nature and priorities of modern life in Cornwall.

From now on the track is fully marked and well documented. The cycle track and footpath down the valley to Pentewan pretty much follows the course of the old railway, so it has a good surface and is almost level all the way. Once, not so long ago, the main road was narrow and dangerous for walkers and cyclists. There was an iron bridge with a nasty little curve, whilst tourist and local traffic inhibited much in the way of exploration. Now it is all opened up, the roads are straighter and wider, the waymarks

CORNWALL'S CHINA CLAY COUNTRY

The White River at Pentewan. Adrian Brown

are down, the footpaths free and unblocked. Kings Woods where once the little trains puffed and struggled are now open to the public, yet few traces of the presence of the tracks can be found. **(F)** In London Apprentice there was a small platform beside a clay dry, and lower down in the woods are traces of sluice ponds that were used to try and keep the harbour free by flushing out the accumulated sands from the river. Boiler Bridge, named after an incident with one of the locomotives near Nansladron, is a popular point of entry to the trail and woods. The banks themselves have been re engineered to stop the once frequent flooding, and since 1973 the White River has officially run clear. All clay-coloured waste water now goes into mica dams or is dealt with on site; woe betide any company that allows the river course to become polluted with clay! In fact the lack of major prosecutions stands up well to the industry taking its position seriously in this respect.

(G) Pentwan Harbour is completely landlocked now; the sand brought down in the White River from Hensbarrow has long since isolated the jetties and landing stages from the open sea. There was a time when the actual beach was dug for gravel, using a small rail-based loader and trucks. The sand was used for ballast and hardcore. The remains of the railway lines and sheds to house the engines are still there, in amongst the yachts and sailing boats stored in the yard.

The White River, now wide and deep enters the sea but its manner and place of crossing the beach changes annually, sometimes close to the old harbour wall, at other times a hundred yards or so away. The white discolouration of the sea that was once such a familiar sight at Pentewan Beach no longer extends out into the bay, although the sand and gravel underfoot still owe much to the china clay industry. This is the end of the White River Pentewan Valley Trail.

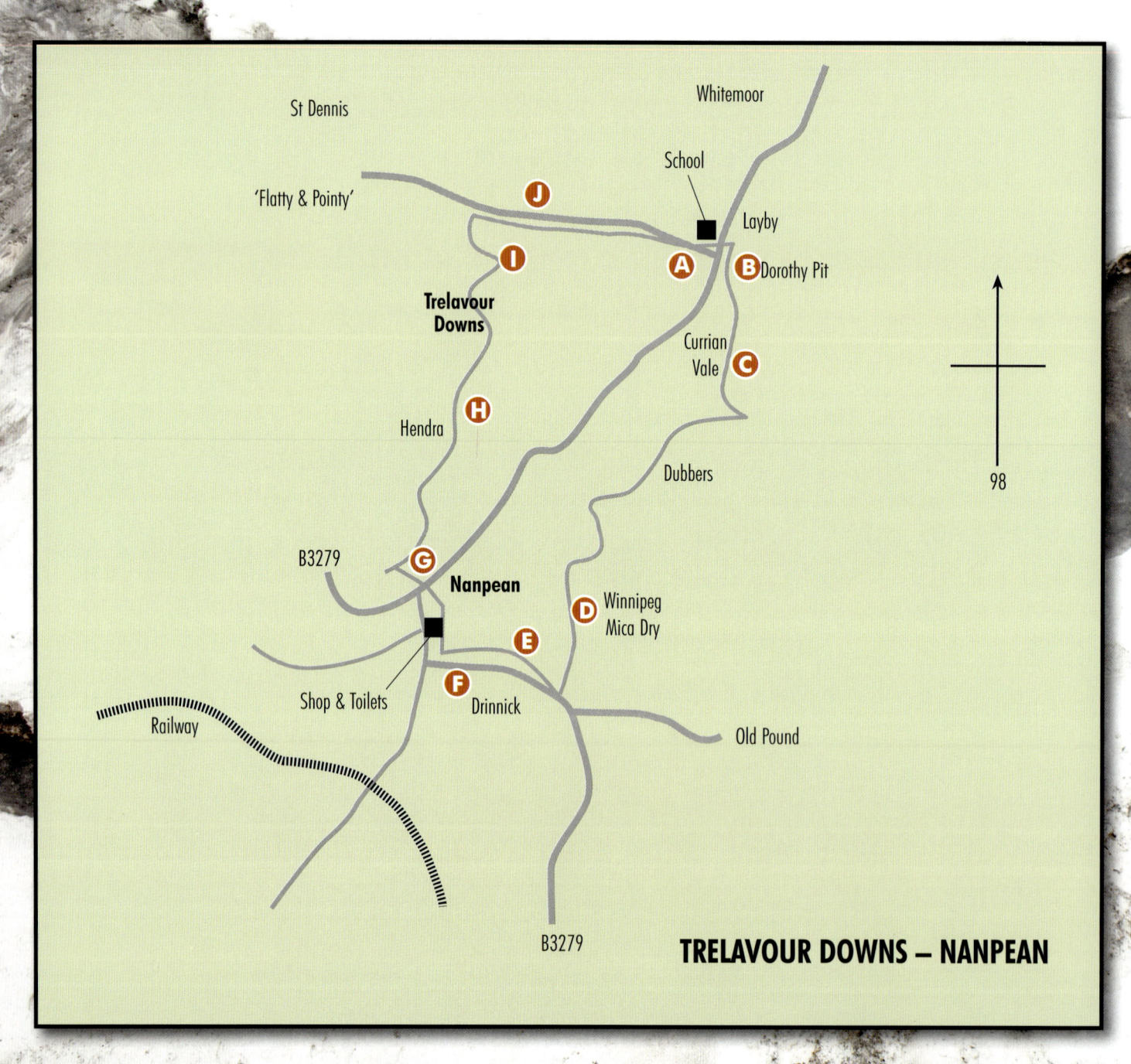

TRELAVOUR DOWNS AND WHITEMOOR TO NANPEAN

THIS IS A CIRCULAR WALK of about 4 miles, starting at Whitemoor School. About half way round there are toilets, a shop and a pub and it is easy to join this walk at many places along the way. The track is mostly well away from the roads, but there are a couple of places where pedestrians have to use the pavement, and the last few hundred yards involve walking along a road back to the start. It's a bit steep and rough in places and not very suitable for buggy-style push chairs. Buses do serve this area from St Austell, but you need to check the times and availability.

(A) In the centre of Whitemoor village there is a parking place on the road to St Dennis outside the Primary School. Please be aware that buses use this space to pick up children from school, so don't block their places. If in doubt park further on up, on the road, or there is a small layby almost opposite the entrance to Dorothy Pit. At the T-junction by

This rare photograph from around 1910 shows the cottages at Karslake. Clearly there was a good community spirit up here in the highest and most windswept part of Hensbarrow. The houses disappeared into the depths of Littlejohns Pit nearly fifty years ago.

C Edyvean

CORNWALL'S CHINA CLAY COUNTRY

At Dorothy Pit a Caterpillar D9 and DW 21 motor scraper are hard at work in 1950.
                                CCHS

The beam engine house at Dorothy in 1910.
                        CCHS

Dorothy, showing the steep incline of the skip track, together with its engine house. Dubbers Tip is in the background.
                        CCHS

28

Adrian Brown's superb aerial photograph reveals the dramatic changes wrought on the landscape by clay mining. Here we look down on the benches at Littlejohns.

Adrian Brown

the school turn left towards Roche and stay on the path used by the schoolchildren to avoid traffic. At the end of the school playing field cross the road where it says 'Imerys Dorothy China Clay Works'. Facing the gates take the path on the right. This is a permissive path and not a public right of way.

Dorothy was so called after Lady Dorothy Fortescue whose family owned the pit. The ancient highway system across these moors no longer exists of course, but the entrance to Dorothy was the start of the way across to Karslake, and anyone could cross the Downs by car to Old Pound, Greensplat or Coldvreath only forty or so years ago from this point. Karslake Cottages, situated at a point not far from the tall mast at Cocksbarrow and accessed by these vanished roads was a windswept and isolated terrace of twelve company-owned houses. They were demolished in the sixties to make way for more mining activities.

(B) Near the entrance to Dorothy are some settling tanks and the reclaimed sand burrows which dominate the village of Whitemoor. Ahead is the vast expanse of Littlejohns Pit. It is hard to imagine how much overburden has been shifted to create a quarry of this size. If you can see into the pit without crossing the fence and there is no mist, then both old and new workings are visible. Overgrown cliffs, new sand roads that have been recently bulldozed and signs of heavy machines working can be observed. The large diameter 'landing' plastic pipe to the side of the wide-haul road carries clay slurry from the pits and settling tanks to the dries. Similar metal pipes carry high pressure water for use in the washing process where clay is blasted out of the rocks using the specially designed monitor hoses.

This is still very much a working environment, although much goes on out of sight away from this immediate area. Follow by eye the lines of pylons and tyre tracks to the distant hills, they lead to what were once separate pits but which have now been carved up to become all part of the same huge operation. Watch out for the muddy and wet catch pits near the fenced path which prevent clay-contaminated water from running off into the naturally occurring streams.

Herbert Truman, 1883-1957, was a Devon Born artist who was a member of the St Ives Society of Artists. Many of his paintings were reproduced as prints and as postcards. This is his impression of Nanpean China clay pit.
C Edyvean

(C) In a few hundred yards the path starts to descend, birds sing and rabbits scurry away. Here, the older indigenous trees compete with introduced species for space to grow. There has been much reclamation and replanting through the China Clay Woodland Project in partnership with Imerys, Natural England and others. £2.5 million has been spent on the clearance of conifers and rhododendrons throughout the clay area, and native broadleaf trees have been planted in their place. An Objective One grant of 80% means that tree species native to Cornwall, mainly oak, ash and birch, together with smaller amounts of mountain ash, holly, hazel and hawthorn now cover much of the waste ground. Trees planted through this project will be recognisable as woodland in a few years time, changing the steep and stark landforms into what should become an attractive and inviting landscape for native plants and animals. Tips are seeded to create a stabilising cover of vegetation. In order to do this job a mulch of grass seed and fertiliser, often mixed with a green dye to identify the areas covered, is sprayed on the tip with a hydroseeding unit mounted on the back of a lorry.

Follow the path keeping the fenced-off high ground to the left. Its difficult to believe how close this is to a busy mine, all around seems so remote and peaceful as the trees close in. There are a number of small copses, ditches full of reeds, wet ground, open fields with black peaty earth that become more overgrown as they get increasingly waterlogged. This is Currian Vale, the high ground to the left is Dubbers mica dam, still in use at the moment. Lower down, near the road, Dubbers merges into the slopes of the much older and disused Winnipeg mica dam. Where this fenced path comes out on to a T-junction turn left on to a much used sand road then go across the cross roads and shortly take the footpath on the left. Although this is marked as a public footpath, no bicycles are allowed, the curious stile arrangement here allows not only the passage of bicycles, even if they have to be lifted over, but also means that horses can jump the low fence. Following this path which takes a high and dry course across some very wet ground, a few signs of a Japanese knotweed infestation may be seen. **(D)** Soon there is a choice of a small bridge or a ford to cross a stream which descends from Old Pound. Take either and keep going straight on, don't turn left or right round the backs of the houses, the path emerges on to the main B3279 right on the outskirts of Nanpean village. Turn right and walk through Nanpean.

The village of Nanpean in the early 1900s before Drinnick had expanded into the fields. The terrace of company-built houses stand in the distance whilst the conical sand burrows are the ones that have been recently landscaped at Hendra and Trelavour. Drinnick has yet to expand into the fields in the foreground.

C Edyvean

The village is justifiably proud of its cemetery which is just on the right. It has won many national awards for its presentation and quality. **(E)** If you wish to pause a while and visit the cemetery, go through the cast iron kissing gate and pass the 1914–919 war memorial. The names on the memorial, which is in the form of an intricately carved granite Celtic cross, are almost all Cornish ones; Bassett, Craddock Hawke, Liddicoat, Rescorla, Teague. Families who still live here and whose names have been associated with the place for centuries. Some of the place names mentioned on the gravestones are occasionally all that remains, the original locations having been demolished or dug up long ago. The church, which was built in 1879, is dedicated to St George the Martyr, the clock over the doorway marks the passing of the hours.

Before the ground was mined there was an opportunity to remove timber from the surface. This is a five-horse team moving trees which have been cut prior to commencing mining operations near Drinnick.
C Edyvean

The immaculate graveyard itself is a haven of peace and tranquility, the paths are swept, the grass is cut and the graves tended. It seems that this is a popular place to be laid to rest because there is a planning application posted for an extension of the burial ground into the field next door. Its status as an outstanding example of a cemetery is recorded on the plaques in the centre of the lawn 'Cemetery of the year awards finalist. For excellence and innovation in management design and customer service'. Those buried here were probably unaware of how much the surrounding area will change in the future, but the reassuring sounds of clay lorries and diggers going past the church may still have some resonance for those interred. Next door to the church are the old churchrooms and Nanpean Primary School.

(F) Across the road from the cemetery is Drinnick. This was very much the heart of operations for ECLP and generations of clay workers. ECLP was the name of the old, pre Imerys Company, the initials stood for English Clays Lovering Pochin & Co, and many people in these parts still refer to the clay company in those terms. Parts of Drinnick are as old as the industry itself. It was the place where fitters and machinists were taught their trades in the engineering department. There were stores and workshops here along with

TRELAVOUR DOWNS AND WHITEMOOR TO NANPEAN

The rail bridge at Goonamarris with Black Five 76079 crossing close to the former generating station and sidings at Drinnick. This type of locomotive would not have seen service in Cornwall, but it serves to illustrate the importance and continuing existence of the mineral branch lines in the area. R Fogg

Below left: *This view of Nanpean taken from Goverseth shows Drinnick Mills Station with Watch Hill and Trelavour Downs on the skyline; this was before extensive tipping covered many of the fields* C Edyvean

Below right: *This view across the playing field at Victoria Bottoms, itself an old pit that had been levelled over to make a football pitch, shows the kilns and electricity generating station at Drinnick in the thirties.* C Edyvean

33

repair and manufacturing facilities, offices and generating stations, railway sidings and loading bays, dries, linhays, settling tanks and all the other accoutrements that go with the industrial hive of activity that it once was. Kettle boys started work here, apprentices learned their trade, shipments were organised, materials recycled. Sadly this is now only a shadow of its former self, and is one of the places that is down for redevelopment with housing and newer industrial premises as part of the Eco Towns scheme.

Pass by Drinnick and keeping to the main road go up the hill, the toilets here are fine, the Post Office is as busy as ever (although only open during the normal working day) and will sell you a snack or a drink. Opposite the Grenville Arms is a small car park and in it is a granite obelisk which the people of Nanpean built to mark the new millennium. Local residents were asked to help with the cost of its construction by sponsoring a brick with their names on, which in turn became part of the monument. Contained within the obelisk is a time capsule with instructions that it is to be opened on the first of January 2100.

(G) Across the road from the pub, just up from the garage, follow the public footpath sign which leads to the rear of some houses and towards a partly-blocked track. It says on a post that the public right of way ends here but don't be deterred by this, just follow the path through the granite boulders keeping the old wall on the left. The land beyond belongs to Imerys and as with the early part of this trail they have given permission for users to walk this way whist retaining the right to close it at any time. This little path comes out on the haul road which almost circumnavigates the flooded Hendra Pit. Turn right, heading uphill and you will come to a cattle grid and a stile arrangement. Be aware that 'haul road' means that; just occasionally a massive dumper may want to share this road with you, just keep well out of the way if you hear it coming!

(H) Above and to the right are the reclaimed open spaces of Trelavour Downs, once all sand burrows and pits but recently landscaped and contoured, reseeded and open for the public to roam about. To the left is Hendra Pit, used as a major mica back-filling operation since 1995, and to the side can be glimpsed older sky tips now completely covered in vegetation. Cattle graze up here; they are used to control invasive and unwanted species and to keep the grass down whilst simultaneously putting a lot of goodness back into the ground. The public has permission to wander about up on the grass and the views of the surrounding countryside are extensive. From the top, if you choose to go up there, can be seen the large complex at Drinnick, the company-built terraced houses in Nanpean and much of the working industrial infrastructure. It's easy from here to see how smaller pits

An early photograph of Hendra Quarry with a general view of china stone working. There appeared to be scant regard for health and safety here, with the undercut cliff looking as if it is about to collapse. CCHS

An AEC Monarch belonging to the Heavy Transport Company being loaded by a Ruston Bucyrus 463 Shovel in 1955.
CCHS

have been subsumed into the newer and larger mines. The remains of an old engine house, once used as a production pumping engine for Trelavour pit, peep out from the undergrowth, and the track that a skip would have taken as it hauled its load from the bottom of the quarry to the top of the sky tip can be easily imagined.

From the cattle grid, stick to the wide gravel road and follow it up to a three-way crossroads where the way bears left, still skirting the edge of the deeply flooded pit. Soon there is a fenced-off area on the left of the track, ignore the pathway that goes along the bottom of the fence and keep the barbed wire on the left. On the way up, and to the left, there is a picturesque little pond that is almost full of bulrushes. Surrounded by small trees and gorse, it is used by cattle as a place to drink. As the path curves left there is a disused overgrown burrow on the right, and on the left a gate through the fence. Do not go through the gate, instead take the washed out and rocky path to the right. This is perfectly fine to walk, rather more challenging to cycle. The cattle make their presence felt underfoot, but they also have made inroads into the undergrowth to seek the lush grass as well as to get shade and shelter. This is a place that has extremes of weather. The winds come in from both coasts, rain comes down a little harder, snow lies deeper and longer and the summer sun can be fierce. Cattle, and people, need to be tough to live and work outside up here!

(I) At the next junction turn left along a waymarked path, there is a line of fencing around a field on the right. Get through the metal barrier somehow, through, round, under or over it. On the left are the remains of clayworks, and there are three prominent skytips, the highest of which are known locally as Flatty and Pointy. For many years the local children have used the base of these two tips as their playground. The village of St Dennis is to the left, the views across this part of Mid Cornwall are breathtaking.

(J) Soon, on the right and through another one of those strange stile arrangements is a small car park at Crown Mine next to the main road between St Dennis and Whitemoor. At this point you have to take to the road and turn right, not for a long distance but it can be a little narrow. This is the outskirts of Whitemoor village, and in a short while you will be back at the village school and the car park where you started.

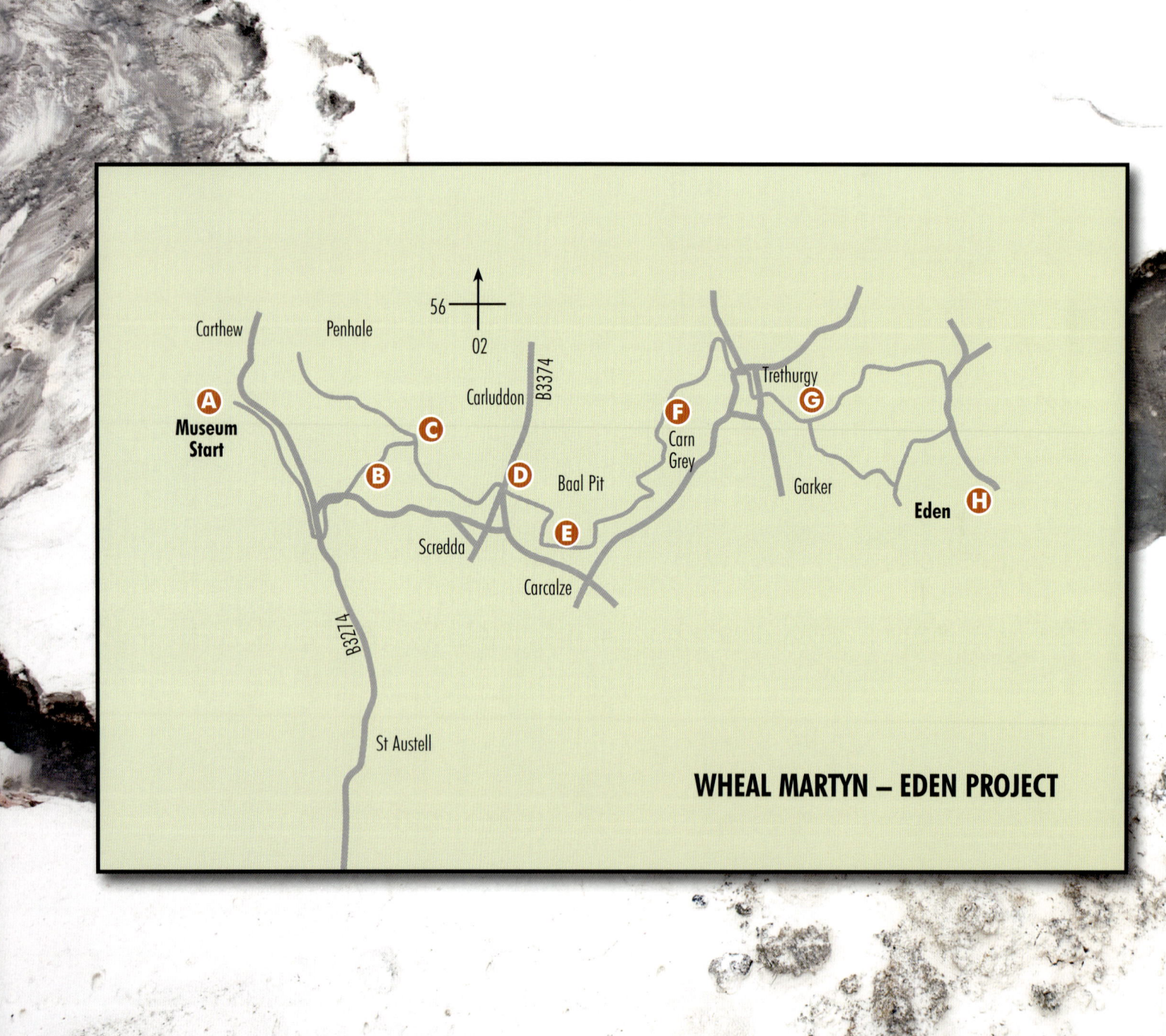

WHEAL MARTYN CHINA CLAY COUNTRY PARK TO THE EDEN PROJECT

THIS IS A FIVE MILE walk or cycle ride and can be joined at many points along its length. There are bus connections to both ends of the walk; parking is readily available at the the Wheal Martyn China Clay Country Park, although Eden firmly closes its gates in the evenings. There is a pub halfway along this trail that provides toilets and refreshments and the surface is suitable for big-tyred pushchairs. The walk takes in extensive views of St Austell Bay together with a closer look at older pits and workings.

(A) From the bottom of Wheal Martyn car park follow the clay trail signs for Eden and St Austell down the slope past Lansalson Pit to Ruddlemoor, all the while staying close to the main road on the trail described in the Trenance Valley chapter. Just after the Cookworthy footbridge the trail divides and the track on the left leads to Eden.

The fields around here, much sought after by owners of ponies, are subject to invasive plants, and attempts to clear the bracken are being made. The trail passes over Drummers Hill which has become something of a rat run in recent years so care must be exercised when crossing. The waymarked gravel path starts to rise through a wooded area with overgrown walls and tumbledown buildings hiding in the undergrowth. Soon it comes to a viewing area on the right. **(B)** This quiet and mysterious lake is Ruddle Pit . It was mined for nearly a hundred years and abandoned in 1935. It is now used as a storage reservoir for Imerys and is deep, dangerous and definitely off-limits to trespassers. When visitors fly over the clay district and into Newquay Airport one of the most noticeable things is the strange colours of the water in the pits. Technical explanations for this are long, but basically the mica that results from mining extraction remains in suspension in the water and reflects the suns rays to spectacular effect. To reclaim the original woodland much of the wild rhododendron that invaded these burrows has been cut back and sprayed with herbicide. Great efforts have been made to encourage birch, oak and ash growth and to

There were numerous waterwheels in the area used for both industrial and farming purposes. The location of this wheel is unknown but it is certainly in the St Austell area. The clay carts were much heavier than this one and usually had a team of three horses to pull them.
C Edyvean

The Eden Project at the former Bodelva Pit. Adrian Brown

get native animals and birds to colonise the newly wooded areas. The water in this holding pit is continuously recycled; it is kept at a certain level using pumps which in turn take it out to where it is to be used and it is also topped up by water which trickles into the pit from natural springs and leats. The trail, gets a little steep just after here and there is a small spur on the right which rejoins the main trail after an alternative look at Ruddle Pit.

(C) At the T-junction the Eden trail goes right. The turning left is a dead end but does have spectacular views back over the Trenance Valley and down towards the Museum. Directly in front, beyond the fence, is what looks to be a jumble of sand, stone and boulders that have been carelessly heaped into great piles with an attempt at replanting and reseeding this area to hide the chaos. In fact these are the sturdily built surrounds of a mica lagoon last used in 2008. The mica in the water would cause instability if it were to be spread on the sand tips. In these lagoons, in effect massive settling tanks, the recycled water was allowed to rest so that much of the mica and other contaminants could sink and

Mica Dry replanting.
Adrian Brown

CORNWALL'S CHINA CLAY COUNTRY

A group of Edwardian clay miners. The Captain, always the one with the bowler hat, was in charge whilst the youngest person there, the kettle boy saw to the everyday food requirements of the group. Generally they had to supply their own clothes so the condition of their working garments was often well worn if not downright ragged.
C Edyvean

John Keay House was the headquarters of English China Clays. It is now part of Cornwall College, but this massive building reflects the importance of the clay industry at the time that it was constructed in the 1960s.
CCHS

build up into a solid mass. In the old days this white water would have been discharged directly into the rivers and taken out to sea, a method of working which of course is no longer acceptable! The surface water was pumped away leaving a flat area contained within the walls which may have been excavated for any remaining good clay and eventually restored to agricultural use.

(D) The trail continues past the village of Scredda, eventually emerging on to the A391 road just above the roundabout at the head of the new distributor road above St Austell. The pub by the roundabout may tempt you down for a coffee or something to eat. After crossing the busy main road the track bears to the right around Baal Pit. At the time of writing this pit is still in its abandoned wild state. Small pumping houses made of corrugated iron sheets and built to run on railway lines, in many ways reminiscent of the skips that were once used here, allows the pumps to be raised or lowered according to the water levels. The prominent conical shaped spoil heap at Carluddon, known to some as 'The Limpet', will be left as it is, it can be seen from way out to sea and provides a Navigation Aid to shipping in St Austell Bay and it also serves as an iconic reminder of how much of the landscape around here once looked; the archetypal 'White Pyramid'.

Baal is one of the places nominated by Imerys as part of their Eco Town bid whereby houses will be built inside the perimeter of the old workings. Again there is much controversy about creating more housing up here, not the least of which is the amount of traffic that will be generated along the narrow and inadequate A391 to Penwithick although the developers are consulting the public on these planning issues. A short way farther on the main trail bears left, but by going through the gate on the right, the whole of St Austell and the Bay comes into view.

There can be days when the wind howls and the rain and mist sweeps in, this can be a very bleak and exposed place, but on fine days the views are extensive. This is a popular place with dog walkers, the large open spaces are ideal for exercising their pets, unfortunately not all are responsible when it comes to cleaning up the mess. Baal Pit has been the location for several films, Dr Who and Spike Milligan have at some stage used this as a background for their antics. Perhaps this is one of the locations that gave the feeling of a moonscape that is so quoted to the point of cliché about the area. There was once a reported incident of a group of councillors on an official visit to the area who observed, from a distance, a pair of large black cat-like animals that were seen basking in the sun in a very remote corner close to here. At the time stories of The Beast of Bodmin Moor were all over the papers and photographs were reputedly taken.

(E) Spread out below is the urban sprawl of St Austell, St Blazey, Par, Tywardreath and Carlyon Bay. This large conurbation has grown enormously since the 1960s, a look at an Ordnance Survey map from 1965 shows open country, hamlets, and villages with fields and winding country lanes where these houses now stand. The new distributor road

Below left: Carclaze Tin Mine was originally dug to get at the tin beneath the ground, only later were there found deposits of china clay. Latterly it became Baal Pit and eventually expanded to encompass much of the ground above Trethurgy. At this site the first of the proposed Eco Town houses will be built.

C Edyvean

Below right: By 1912 Carclaze Clay works had developed out of the tin mine and was producing serious amounts of clay.

C Edyvean

CORNWALL'S CHINA CLAY COUNTRY

Carclaze dry with wagons and horses waiting to load. This dry still exists and has been converted into industrial units. It is close to the top of the new St Austell distributor road at Carclaze.
CCHS

seems to form some kind of a boundary to the housing development but the open fields above the town await planning applications for more homes, whilst the Brewery looks as if it is about to be surrounded by a new estate. Tregonnissey, the village just below, is where A. L. Rowse the noted local Shakespearian scholar and poet and the author of *A Cornish Childhood* went to school. It has now become completely absorbed into the main town and the old saw mills nearby where a local speedway ace could tune his bikes at full throttle knowing that few people could hear or complain has become full of newly built houses. Supermarkets have appeared where cows once grazed and a redundant clay dry has been converted into luxury flats.

Away in the distance the sea has not changed, except for the absence of the small fleet of coasters patiently waiting for high tide and a berthing space in Par, Charlestown or Fowey Harbours where they could take on their cargoes of clay bound for foreign shores. The daymark on the Gribbin is clearly visible, as is Black Head with its little house that can only really be reached by sea. St Austell Bay can be followed until it reaches the Dodman, whilst the coastline can be traced along the Roseland and as far as St Mawes. In another chapter we shall look at the ports and some of the other parts of the town in more detail.

(F) Moving on towards the village of Trethurgy, the trail parallels the old main road, Four Stones Hill, leading to Luxulyan until it gets to the stone quarry at Carn Grey. The open spaces around Carn Grey Tor provide ample opportunities for less constrained wanderings, and at the top distant glimpses of Helman Tor and the Luxulyan valley can be seen, along with views of Penwithick village. Before the last war the boulders of Carn Grey Tor were in danger of being blasted out of existence by an extension of the stone quarry; in those days it was just another heap of hardcore that represented an easy profit, and only spirited resistance by local people stopped this from happening

Below left: *A view of Trethurgy from Carn Grey. It shows Alseveor and the working buildings of the stone quarry. This is close to the site of the excavated Roman Round which was later buried under the spoil from Baal Pit.*

C Edyvean

Below right: *Carn Grey dominates the skyline near Trethurgy. Right beside it was and still is, a stone quarry. It was only through the intervention of Dr A L Rowse and others that stopped the Tor being blown up and used as just more roadstone.*

C Edyvean

The administrative buildings on the edge of the Eden Project can now be seen, and the end is in sight, with most of the rest of the journey downhill. Numerous access points to the trails go off into the surrounding countryside, leading to villages or car parks. During the early seventies when the tipping at Carn Grey was due to begin, a rescue archaeological dig was organised. It had been known for some time that there was evidence of a settlement here. In 1973, under the leadership of Henrietta Quinnell, an excavation revealed a 'round', a type of small enclosed settlement of considerable status prevalent in Cornwall from the late Iron Age until the early post Roman period. After carefully examining the site, an extremely detailed report was written, and then the remains were covered in plastic and eventually buried underneath the spoil heaps. The report can still be obtained from Cornwall Council (ISBN 1 903798 12 4).

CORNWALL'S CHINA CLAY COUNTRY

A newly instated Clayliner train pulled by class 47 D1670 Mammoth leaves St Austell on its way to Kent with tanker loads of china clay. This photograph was taken on Carlyon Bay Golf Course in the sixties; the fields below the skyline are now full of houses. CCHS

The heathland has been encouraged to regenerate, it is an important habitat for rare and endangered species such as adders, nightjars and stonechats. It is not always possible to see such rarities, but usually pairs of buzzards can be seen hunting for their prey amongst the bracken and small trees which have been planted on the reprofiled slopes. Again just watch for the little red arrows that are the waymarks, sometimes they are hard to see. Near Trebal catch-pits turn right on to the tarmac road to Trethurgy following the signs, go left, then right again until you reach the Old Trethurgy Chapel where the trail turns left along a sandy track. All around amongst the trees, bushes and marshland can be seen the evidence of man's presence over the centuries. This is the top of Garker Valley, which has not been used for the production of clay for many years.

(G) There is an open space at the end of this track. To the left can be glimpsed a pond beyond a steel gate. This is an old quarry that is private property and not to be touched, anglers only are allowed with licences! There is then a choice of routes to take, both lead to The Eden Project. The right hand track will end up in one of the car parks whilst straight ahead is the shortest way and although it is a bit narrow and rough underfoot it will bring you out on to the main entrance road.

A small diversion here is to cross this road by the cattle grid and take the bridleway on the other side. This will eventually take you out on to the Luxulyan road close to the back entrance of Eden. Beware though, after a mostly dry and firm surface so far, this really is an ancient track. It can be narrow, wet and brambly yet it represents a less sanitised but equally appealing version of the tracks used in past times by workers in the clay industry. **(H)** Now have a cup of coffee or something in the cafeteria, and relax, that's quite a good walk!

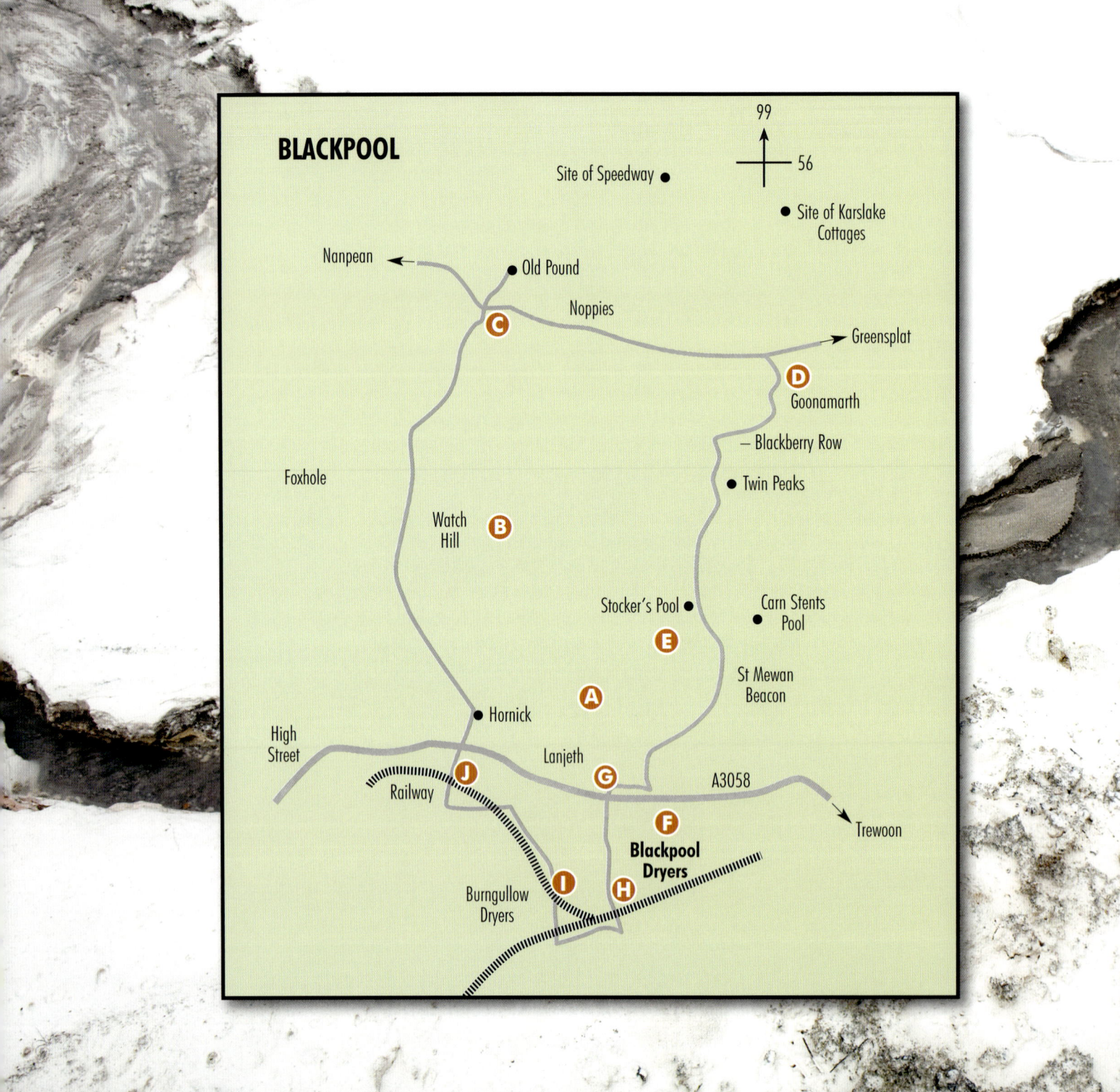

BLACKPOOL PIT

THIS WALK CAN BE circular or it can be divided up into several parts. The biggest problem when completing the circle is a short stretch of very busy main road in Lanjeth where there is no pavement. Locals use the road to get to the shops, but you may wish to retrace your footsteps in order to avoid this bit. There are three designated car parks along the way, and other places where leaving a vehicle is not a problem. There are no toilets and the entire walk is around five miles, although much shorter sections of a mile or so can be done by returning along the way you have just come. A further difficulty for cyclists and those with prams, is that the design of the kissing gates at the top and bottom of the first part of the Blackpool Trail makes it difficult to get through, however the public

Another of the smaller pits subsumed into the vast Blackpool complex. This is a Ruston Bucyrus 19RB shovel loading a dumper in the freezing cold winter of 1962/3. Imagine what it was like to be the hoseman at this time!

CCHS

BLACKPOOL PIT

Mica particles in suspension refract the light causing the startling colours in the pool at Blackpool Pit.

Adrian Brown

road runs parallel with it and can be used as an alternative. The complete walk takes in the whole of the Blackpool complex to enable the observer to understand how the operation worked. It's a big place which includes the flooded pit, the sand burrows, the dryers and the railway sidings, so it is perfectly possible to attempt only parts of the walk and then come back to do the rest at another time.

It is important when walking around Blackpool to have some knowledge and understanding of the recent history of the pit. The solid ramparts of the tips rise from the ground above the village of Lanjeth like a medieval fortress, dominating the landscape for miles around. These slopes along with the conical sky tips seem to personify the China Clay area and define the Southern boundaries of the clay producing district. They may seem in imminent danger of sliding away, but their 'angle of repose' is such that they cannot move on their own without outside influence.

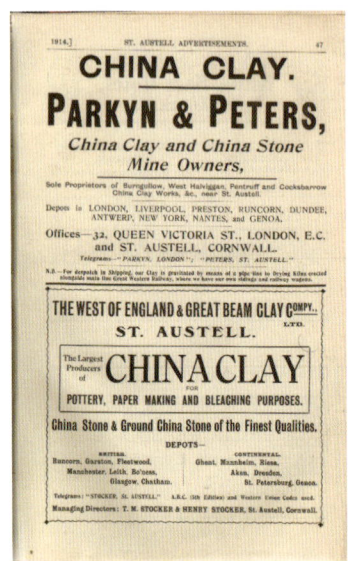

China Clay adverts from 1914. The director of the West of England & Great Beam Clay Company, Medland Stocker, played a principal role in getting the 1913 strike broken. He was the Stocker in the BBC play 'Stocker's Copper'.
C Edyvean

When it was announced by Imerys in 2006 that Blackpool Pit was to be closed the following year, 177 years of continuous mining operations came to an end at that particular site. Reasons cited were that it had become uneconomic to continue production due to reduced foreign demand for the Cornish product, the volatile money markets and the geological nature of Brazilian clay which made it far more economic for the paper-coating sectors to get their products from South America. The unions were unhappy, many workers became redundant and a complete range of buildings and general infrastructure was now no longer needed. Despite protestations work in the pit gradually came to an end.

Operations within the pit primarily depend upon a dry environment, and this is provided by the continuous running of water drainage pumps. When they are switched off the whole area starts to become saturated by the many springs and watercourses that naturally empty into the depths of the quarried areas. All existing fixings have to be recovered, there is an amazing assortment of items that accumulate as part of the mining activities. From conveyor belts to tin sheds, monitors to Portakabins, old bits of pipe to electricity poles, they all have to be taken out. The inevitable flooding of the deepest parts of the pit mean that inexorably the water creeps ever higher up the sides of the workings. Wide tracks that just a few weeks earlier had seen the passage of dumper trucks and Land Rovers now look like boat launching ramps; drowning bushes and small trees peep from the surface of the water whilst the cliffs and steep-sided slopes take on the appearance of some remote Rocky Mountain waterhole.

And of course this was not the only change; other, more subtle things happened. For one thing the lights went out. For as long as people could remember the bright glow of the sodium lights throughout the night lit up the works and the countryside around. Twenty-four hours a day Blackpool operated and the settling tanks and dries, the loading areas and the rail sidings were fully illuminated. The paths of the conveyor belts could be traced as they took the sand to be dumped on the tips, and the headlights of the Land Rovers swept the night sky. Now the electricity was turned off and quietness and darkness descended over the area. No longer was the sound of reversing trucks to be heard, no more would the sound of the sirens wailing prior to blasting be heard, the short sharp concussive effect and the slight tremor in the ground be felt. The wind-blown dust storms emanating from the tips gradually decreased, the steam from the slurry plant stopped, the hum and crackle of the electricity stations and the background whirr of the presses and the furnaces came to a halt.

The once all-white appearance of the buildings began to change to a darker colour as the mosses, lichens, brambles and small gorse bushes started to take hold. Security fences, railings and boarded-up buildings became dominant where once the bustle of a busy industrial process was all that was important. Blackpool Pit and all its associated buildings were no longer required for the mining and refining of what was once regarded as the finest china clay in the world.

(A) The 5 mile walk around Blackpool begins at the car park at the bottom of the 'Blackpool Trail' and is reached by turning off the A3058 at the crossroads near the layby in Lanjeth and going up Hornick Hill about 100 yards. The car park is on the right and the track starts at the kissing gate where it immediately starts to climb up beside the sand burrow. Beneath the huge depths of waste sand at this point lie the remains of several houses and bungalows which formed part of the hamlet of Hornick. They belonged to the Clay Company and, as soon as the land was required for tipping, the dwellings were emptied and then simply covered over as they stood. Outbuildings, gardens, even old vehicles were just buried there for ever.

As the path rises steeply, walkers become aware of the height of the tips and the views from the track. This is Watch Hill, one in a series of high points that stretched all the way to London where once beacons were prepared, ready to be lit in case of Spanish Invasion. **(B)** Towards the top of the hill are seats and an inscribed slate stone that gives the names and direction of significant locations in the far distance. St Agnes Beacon, Carn Brea and The Lizard can all be observed as can the high ground beyond St Ives on a clear day,

A Peerless lorry belonging to Richards & Sharp was the prize winner at Indian Queens Carnival in the early twenties. Note all the local connections, Wheal Remfry Bricks, Cornish Mines, H D Pochin & Co, and the Cornish AF registration number.
CCHS

This family group owned a smallholding near Old Pound. They farmed their few acres whilst at the same time the man would go off to his day job in the clayworks.
C Edyvean

CORNWALL'S CHINA CLAY COUNTRY

Soay sheep on a replanted tip. Adrian Brown

perhaps 40 miles away. The south coast is visible from St Austell Bay right around the Dodman and on down towards the Roseland and St Mawes. The main railway line can be followed as it winds its way from St Austell down towards Truro, through the Coombe Valley and across the viaduct beyond.

On the sides of Blackpool pit have been planted many trees in the expectation that they will grow up and hide the scars of the waste tips. They are protected from predating rabbits by plastic tubes but on the bleak windswept slopes some of the saplings are losing the fight for survival, this is a harsh environment indeed. If the land is left alone scrub, gorse, brambles and small thorns tend to take over. In an attempt to prevent this happening a flock of Soay sheep was introduced into the environs of the tip to keep the grass and other invasive plants down. They are particularly suited to this kind of land, easily managing the steep rough ground, they breed readily and are tough enough to survive the winters. The sheep are light footed so tend not to damage any fenced off pre-seeded ground over which they might inadvertently wander. The Soays are looked after by a shepherd, but are still semi wild and roam about all over the place. There are times when a little group of sheep get out of the fenced areas of the pit and on to the roads or into people's gardens, but fortunately these occurrences are rare.

A bit farther along the track there are distant views out towards the north coast but there are also ample opportunities to look at the villages of Foxhole, St Stephen, and Nanpean. This is a good chance to observe how the old and the new china clay works, new housing developments, older conical tips and modern landscaped areas intermingle. The older housing developed in a linear fashion, following the major roads and supporting the kinds of shops and houses that fitted in with the pattern of the clay works. In Foxhole, as in most of the other villages in the area, there is no tradition of the village green with attendant pub, church, school and village shop. All these components exist but are strung out along the road which carried the clay traffic. They are supplemented by former blacksmiths' shops, wheelwrights, cooperages, stables and the like that would have supported those engaged in the industry. In more recent times these have been replaced by small hauliers' yards, garages, builders and engineering works.

The older pattern of agriculture can also be noted. In the lower lands away from the china clay villages traditional farming was carried on, the farms and fields that have developed over the centuries readily bear this out. However closer to the clay works much smaller and more ancient dwellings and field patterns exist side-by-side with the pits and sand burrows. These smallholdings would have consisted of a few acres, big enough to keep a cow, some pigs, perhaps hay fields, sufficient at least to supplement the clay workers' earnings without having to entirely depend on the mines for a living wage. Along the hedges of the road that parallels the trail could, indeed still can, be found what are locally known as 'erts', whortleberries, that when picked can be made into the most delicious of pies.

The Blackpool Trail continues on to some crossroads at Old Pound. Here lie buried the remains of the former Foxhole Cricket Club, and a substantial farmhouse and outbuildings that were demolished to make the new road. There is a car park here, the other end of The Blackpool Trail and this is one of the points where walkers may wish to turn around and go back again; alternatively the way continues by turning right along the tarmac road at a place called Noppies.

(C) 'The New Road' is so called by older locals because it replaced a system of highways which once connected the local villages across the top of the moors. In the old days the dead end leading to Littlejohns would have taken the traveller on across the moors to Karslake, Whitemoor and Roche. During the sixties and seventies all these roads disappeared as the ground was cleared when a huge superpit was created. The village of Karslake, company owned, was bulldozed to the ground and only memories and photographs now show that it even existed. Places with names like Shilton and Vinegar Point were lost, the open moors became deep pits, and few traces of any houses exist, although there are some ruined cottages where cows graze in former vegetable gardens and where pastures have been left for the brambles and ferns to take over. From 2001-2003 part of Littlejohns was used by Trelawny Tigers speedway team as their track. They were part of the British Premier League and the Clay Country Moto Parc was a 230 metre track renowned for its quality of preparation and the racing it produced. Although this was largely successful and crowds of spectators came to watch their favourite teams do battle on the oval, it did not last long because the company wanted to reclaim the land for further clay excavations. Whilst the speedway lasted the visual effects could be quite magical, the floodlights lit up the surrounding cliffs, and hills and the arena took on the appearance of an ancient Roman amphitheatre, with leather clad riders taking the place of gladiators.

Over the crest of the hill at Noppies, on what can be quite a busy road, are the first glimpses of the newly flooded Blackpool pit. It will have taken around four years for the water to reach the top and start to spill over, for those who cannot imagine its depths, you only have to look at the amount of spoil left over and think about where it came from.

BLACKPOOL PIT

*A long-since demolished 46 ½"
rotative beam engine at Blackpool.*
CCHS

CORNWALL'S CHINA CLAY COUNTRY

An historic photograph of Parkyns Deep with Wheal Louisa. This is one of the many smaller pits that went to make up the much larger Blackpool Pit.

CCHS

Foxglove.

Adrian Brown

Walk half a mile, mostly downhill, along the 'New Road' as far as a footpath on the right just on a bend, then follow the path past a ruined farm and on to a track where a left turn brings you out on to another tarmac road. **(D)** This is another of the lost hamlets, Goonamarth. Once there was a small community of people who lived here at Blackberry Row, now all trace of human habitation has gone and the through road ends in a pile of boulders put there to prevent would be off-roaders trying their chances.

Continue past a disused sky tip, known as Twin Peaks covered in heathers and gorse, where the concrete remains of the bridge that carried the skip still stand. Blackpool has a long and interesting history, enough stories could be told about the place to make a small book! The road continues across moorland, to the left are views of Gover Valley and distant glimpses of St Austell. Soon the way bears right and the village of Trewoon can be seen, accessed by Carne Hill on the left. A track to the right leads to St Mewan Beacon, a small outcrop of rock that is overshadowed by the settling tanks and buildings of Blackpool. Here again there are some wonderful views down the Pentewan Valley and to Sticker and Polgooth, whilst further on is Gorran water tower and St Ewe. South Polgooth, Ventonwyn and Dowgas engine houses can be seen, although these were of course used for the underground mining of tin..

(F) Below the fields and the fir trees can be seen the vast redundant complex, Blackpool Dryers, which was a clay drying plant. Although it stopped work in 1985, at its peak it produced twelve thousand tonnes of clay per week. This whole area is the site of Imerys' application for one of their Eco Towns. There are plans by an Egyptian-led consortium to turn the redundant works and fields which straddle the main Newquay to St Austell road at Blackpool into a futuristic community of 2500 new houses, shops, schools, and a station. There are mixed views locally about these plans. Many feel an obvious need to find alternative uses for the old buildings and brown-field sites that remain as a result of the mines closures. Plans to build a whole new town with all the implications for existing

The construction of the silos at Blackpool Dryers in 1965. These never worked properly, the clay tended to jam up and would not run freely from the chutes at the bottom.

CCHS

CORNWALL'S CHINA CLAY COUNTRY

Burngullow station and the branch line to Parkandillack. This aerial shot was taken before the dryers were built alongside the main line and show the kilns of Parkyn and Peters together with Tehidy Minerals works.

CCHS

Diesel Electric locomotive Class 37-4 number D6990 'Caerphilly Castle' on the Clay Pony Special train passing one of the last loads to be taken out of Burngullow Dryers sidings at Crugwallons in 2006.

R. Fogg

communities may be going too far. Questions about what work will be available, what will happen to the sewage, how will all the other villages and road networks cope with an influx of thousands of new arrivals, what will happen to the character of the people who have lived there for hundreds of years are asked. There is undoubtedly a need for more housing, extra work and the raising of income levels in the area but still the plans are controversial and it remains to be seen how much comes of them.

Here is another place where you may wish to park your car and retrace your footsteps. **(G)** To continue the walk carry on down the hill, pass the sand plant on the right and at the bottom take the main A3085 to the right. This piece of road is very narrow and busy, without benefit of a pavement for almost a hundred yards although there are green verges that can be used, so take particular care here. Turn left off the main road down Burngullow Lane

If you are tired and want to get back to the start then you can do so but only by walking further along the main road. It's very dangerous here, and great care has to be taken as the traffic is fast and there is little shelter from it. This is a real problem to residents of Lanjeth as their nearest shop is in Trewoon and the only way to get there on foot is to run this particular gauntlet of hazardous highway. In 100 yards or so, on the right there is a pavement which goes through Lanjeth to the bottom of Hornick Hill. The car park at the start is just up the hill from there.

Having turned down Burngullow lane, go past the back entrance of Blackpool Dryers, now fenced off, and the ruined chimney which marks the entrance to what was once the station at Blackpool. **(H)** The remains of a weighbridge can be seen in the road , and the freight depot which is still the main marshalling point for all the railbound clay traffic from the western area is visible from the railway bridge. This is of course the main London Penzance line, but it also marks the junction of the Parkandillack branch; loaded trains still descend the line very carefully. There is a lot of weight behind the locomotives as they make their way down from the hills. Perhaps the drivers remember that day in 1952 when a loaded train smashed through the level crossing gates, its brakes having failed. The fireman leapt from the cab into some brambles and was saved; the driver stayed with his train and careered under this bridge. Nothing could be done to avoid a collision with the loaded trucks in the sidings, the train was wrecked and the driver killed.

The huge, now redundant dries awaiting demolition can be seen to good advantage from this bridge. The groups of silos here, built to contain powdered clay never worked

BLACKPOOL PIT

properly, the clay just would not flow freely and would constantly jam up. After the bridge go on a little way then turn sharply right before the farm. In a while turn right towards Lanjeth and go back over two railway bridges again. **(I)** The chimney stack on the overgrown clay dry which used clay from Longstone Pit has FP 1927 cast on it. FP is the initials of its then owner, Frank Parkyn. Next comes the boarded up Burngullow dryers, (Burngullow, not to be confused with bungalow, from the Cornish Bron, hill; Gollow, light) which are also awaiting the bulldozer. Bear left here and peek through the wooden fence at the only recently abandoned buildings that house the presses and dryers. Safety notices remain over disused settling tanks with their access ladders cut away, and the redundant conveyor belt no longer squeaks its way across the road with powdered clay ready to be stored then loaded into the lorries from the linhay.

Crugwallons Dry at Burngullow. Note the all-pervasive covering of white dust.
CCHS

Continue along the road beside the branch line passing the converted chapel, then turn left and once again cross the railway bridge. **(J)** In a short while bear right and then start up the hill over the unmanned level crossing. Cross over the main road and the car park at the start is just up the hill on the right.

Blackpool Pit in the final stages of operation in 2008. The pit is already beginning to flood yet even at this late stage monitors are still blasting clay out of the rocks and dumpers are hauling overburden to the burrows. All the buildings, poles and conveyor belts will soon have to be moved as the water slowly but surely begins to rise. R. Fogg

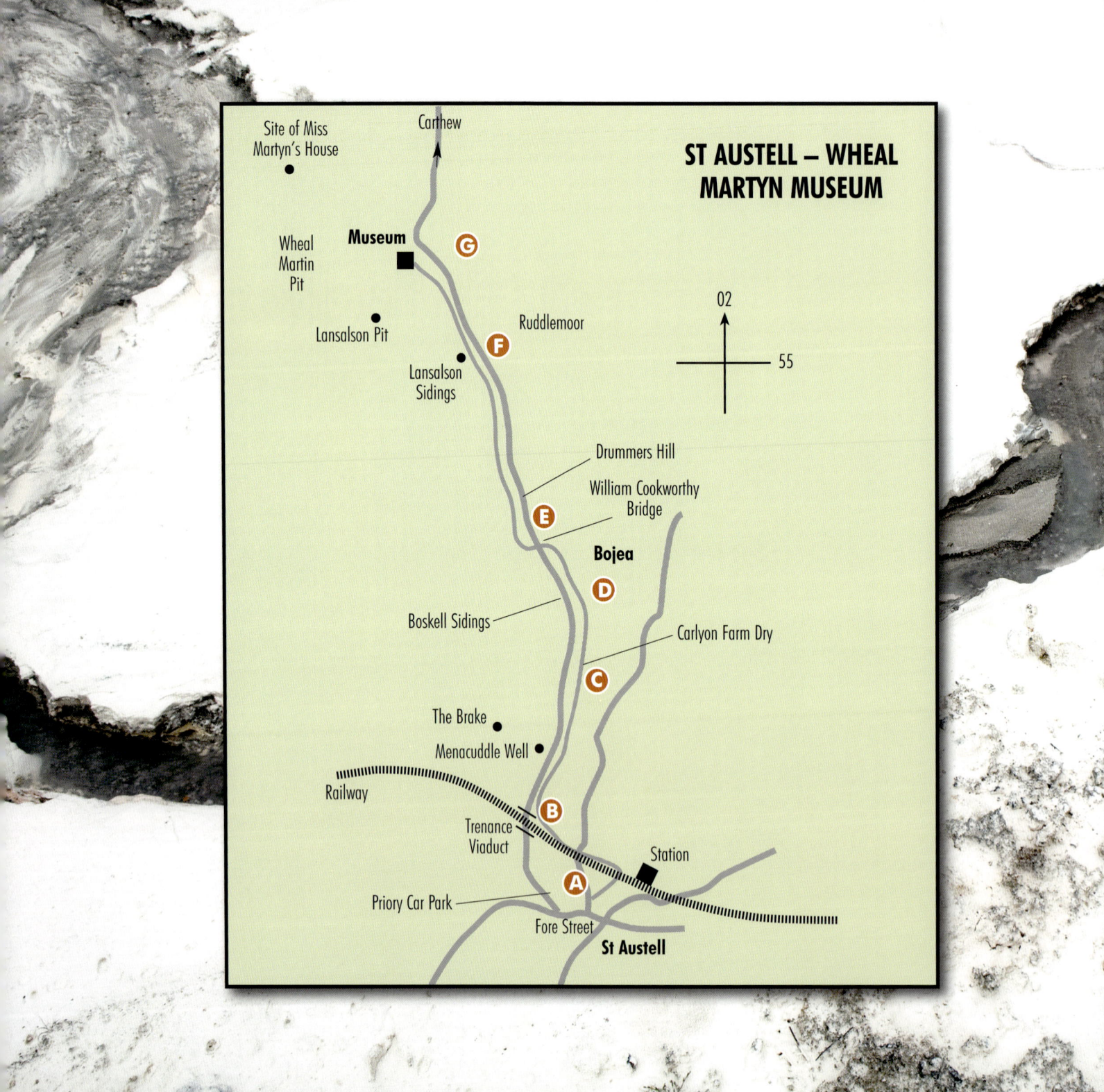

THE BOJEA BRANCH, ST AUSTELL TO WHEAL MARTYN MUSEUM

THIS WALK, LESS THAN two miles in length, follows the path of the old branch line up the Trenance Valley as far as The China Clay Country Park at Ruddlemoor. It is an ideal prelude to a visit to the museum and gives an opportunity for a fairly level walk through some of the older workings close to the town of St Austell. It's easily done by bicycle and push chair. There is plenty of parking space in St Austell, or if you want to do it in reverse at the Museum.

All horse-drawn clay traffic was routed through the main street of St Austell. The resultant mess and damage was the source of many complaints.

CCHS

CORNWALL'S CHINA CLAY
COUNTRY

Spoil being removed (Fal Valley) St Dennis and Parrandillick in the distance.

Adrian Brown

St Austell was always the business centre of the clay industry. There are those who feel that proclamations on signs citing it as 'An Ancient Market Town' should be amended to 'Ancient Mining Town'. Throughout the town were established the various offices, hotels, pubs, shops and other businesses that were necessary to support the burgeoning china clay industry which was developing in the 19th century. The architecture of Fore Street still reflects the style of these former shops, although behind the main street there has been some recent serious development in terms of the White River Place. This replaced a lot of buildings that were built in the 1960s but which proved inadequate for twenty-first century requirements. Much more information about St Austell can be found on various websites, the tourist information office and the informative St Austell Discovery Map.

The main street, narrow as it is, was the main thoroughfare for the wagonloads of clay coming down the Trenance Valley en route to the ports of Charlestown, Pentewan or Par. It is recorded that visitors to the town commented on the mess that was left behind from both the wagons and the horses. At the opposite end of Fore Street from the Church, on the sharp corner was a pub called The General Wolfe, it is now a toy shop. The pub occupied the whole corner, and the thirsty wagon drivers coming down the Trenance Valley with their loads of clay would buy their beer from the top window, and by the time they were round the corner they could hand in the empty glass at the bottom window without pausing on their journey. Some of the loads were destined for the Pentewan Railway, covered in another chapter, and would make the steep trip down West Hill to the terminus with the assistance of iron shoes or drags on the cartwheels to stop them running away. Bulk clay, or clay that was packed in barrels or casks weighing around 250kg (5cwt), caused the combined weight of the steel-tyred wagons and the hooves of the horses to take its toll on the structure of the road. This method of transport was slow and the relatively long distances between the point of production and the ports made the construction of a mineral railway from the main line up the valley to Ruddlemoor a viable and less expensive alternative. The new railway was constructed in 1920 starting not far from St Austell Station, branching off the main line just before Brunel's Trenance Valley viaduct and going at first to Bojea then on to Lansalson which is very close to the site of the present China Clay Country Park.

(A) To begin this trail, start by the Church and take the small road, North Street, up behind the Market House. Keep going uphill and cross the railway bridge over the Plymouth to Penzance main line. Turn left and near the end of Tremena Road there is a small sign on the left by the viaduct indicating the narrow cycle path and clay trail to Bojea and the Clay Country Park. The large Victorian villas along this road were built by people who had a

THE BOJEA BRANCH, ST AUSTELL TO WHEAL MARTYN MUSEUM

Trenance, Brunel's viaduct before 1890 showing the Baltic pine upper sections carried on stone piers. The wood was constantly reinforced because the weight of the trains could make the rails spread if they were left unwatched.

C Edyvean

In this photograph of Trenance Viaduct, the Bojea branch line has still not been built. On the main Bodmin Road out of St Austell there were many businesses powered by water wheels using leats diverted from the river. This is the narrow road that carried so much clay traffic and it is easy to see why a replacement railway line would have been such an attractive proposition.

C Edyvean

financial stake in the industry, mine captains, bankers, even pit owners lived in these flamboyant and stylish houses.

For those who might have some difficulty in finding the start, another option is to go straight up from the Priory car park through the Priory grounds, passing the Audiology Centre. In the top right hand corner is a short alleyway which comes out just below the Railway Bridge and Tremena Road.

(B) Close-up views from the path of the railway viaduct over the Trenance Valley give an idea of how the original bridge, designed and built by Brunel, was replaced by an all-stone construction. The remains of the original piers, still firm and strong but covered in ivy and small bushes, stand alongside those in present use. On each pier was constructed sets of diagonally braced timber struts which radiated upwards and carried massive beams with the decking for the railway lines. The original was 115 feet high, 720 feet long and had 10 piers. Brunel knew when he made his wooden viaducts there was only a limited number of years that they could be used before they would need major maintenance, or complete replacement. They never failed, although they looked fragile and had to be constantly maintained. Sometimes they had to be shored up to stop the lines themselves spreading under the weight of the heavy trains passing over. Eventually the existing all-stone replacement was built in 1899 and it is still in use today. This was the scene of one of St Austell's darker moments. In 2007 three people were convicted and jailed for the murder of Steven Hoskin by forcing him to jump to his death from this bridge, a murder which shocked and appalled everyone in the area, and which had far reaching consequences for the way people with learning difficulties were treated in the county.

Just beyond the viaduct on the far side was a small siding which has now fallen out of use, but the Bojea branch departed from the main line more or less at the beginning of the bridge. The remains of the old wooden fence posts mark the side of the track as it descended steeply for a while before levelling out and crossing a small road which bisects the trail. Below is the main Bodmin Road which leads from the town up the valley to Stenalees, Bugle and Roche and passes the China Clay Museum, whilst Menacuddle Well, a spring with a small stone building where there was once a medieval chapel, is only accessible from the road. Beneath the viaduct, and in fact all along the sides of this track, can be seen the remains of water mills which were used mainly for the more traditional purposes of grinding corn or powering industrial machinery rather than clay-related work. Across the valley in the woods can be seen The Brake, an old mansion house which is now a retirement home and which is close to the source of all the fresh water that is used in St Austell Brewery. The Brewery is only just over the hill above St Austell, but cannot be seen from the trail

Carlyon Farm Dry with narrow gauge wagons full of still warm clay from the floor of the dryer being tipped into the mainline wagons. This was known as 'tramming'.

CCHS

(C) Continuing towards Bojea the trail is a gradual upward incline, the path is firm and wide, but is sometimes lightly flooded by streams coming down from the steep valley sides. Soon there appears on the right a large concrete building. This is Carlyon Farm Dries. It is larger than many similar types but follows the traditional pattern. It may seem that the structure in the middle once housed one of the old beam engines, but in fact this was where the furnaces were, the grate doors can still be seen hanging from rusty hinges. The heat generated dried the clay and exited through the two chimneys at either end of the abandoned buildings. Clay wagons would be shunted into the siding next to these high walls. Sweating labourers would tip the dried clay which had been shovelled from the heated floor into little railway trucks which ran from the interior of the building, straight out into the waiting wagons. The place lacks the romantic appeal that so many old clay works have; it feels more like a Second World War bunker that has not yet acquired the patina of time. Ferro concrete is the dominant material, rusty pipework and fallen branches its accompaniment. There was an application recently to convert this building into a hotel and conference centre, it was turned down.

A kiln furnace with the sliding doors open ready to receive a fresh supply of coal.
CCHS

Below: *Trethowel kiln, mica drags and tanks, with Carlyon Farm beyond.*
CCHS

Bottom: *Carlyon Farm Dry in 1932 with central press house and furnace. The main Bodmin road runs up the valley, hidden below the railway line which is now part of the Bojea Clay Trail.*
CCHS

(D) Not far along the trail, the path skirts around the small Bojea Industrial Estate which has been built across the former track bed. Just beyond the factory units the railway would have crossed the Bodmin Road on a granite bridge, this was demolished to help ease traffic congestion. Low bridges like this, as was the case of the bridge on the Goss Moor, are vulnerable to increased load height on modern vehicles. The clay trail goes up through steep fields and over a brand new bridge, constructed for pedestrians and cyclists to cross a lane leading to Bojea farm. The views up and down the valley are beginning to open up here, Directly in front are the green acres of the China Clay Country Park and beyond the works at Gunheath. The mature trees on the skyline at Wheal Martyn stand out in contrast to the almost impenetrable infestation of rhododendrons that cloak the abandoned spoil heaps in the lower part of the valley. Once, up there, was a wood with

Above: *Boskell siding near Bojea just before it was closed to rail traffic taken in 1964. The main road from Stenalees to St Austell runs on the other side of the wooden fence. In the distance is Wheal Martyn, the site of the present day museum.*
C Edyvean

Above right: *The process of shovelling the dried clay from the heated floors of the kilns and putting it into small carts was known as 'tramming'. The clay was then put into a linhay where it was stored prior to onward shipping.*
C Edyvean

the bluest of bluebells, the loudest of birdsongs and the prettiest of shortcuts in and around Miss Martyn's house at Carthew. The house was the property of the family that had owned and worked the pit for many years. Now all that has been swept away, bulldozed to get at the valuable minerals beneath. There is just enough of the original landscape within the bounds of the museum to get an idea of what it was once like.

After the detour around the industrial units, the trail separates the fields from tumbledown granite walls overlooking the road, then in a short distance the way divides. Onwards is Eden, but the way to the Country Park turns sharp left, down and back. After cutting through the sides of an ancient circular stone-built settling tank, the trail crosses the main road on the aptly named William Cookworthy Bridge. **(E)** Cookworthy was of course the founding father of the clay industry, in 1748 he found large deposits of kaolin in the St Austell area and opened a small pottery in Plymouth to manufacture porcelain, after which commercial extraction of clay started in earnest. From the bridge, looking down you may just be able to pick out the remains of Boskell siding. The old railway bed now rejoins the trail and continues parallel with the road through another group of deserted buildings that once served the railway and which were used for drying, storage and loading purposes. Where a farm track crosses the trail there can be found two sets of railway tracks still buried in the ground. **(F)** This marks the start of Lansalson sidings, the highest point at which the railway reached. In place of the loading ramp which has been demolished, there is a long narrow lawned area that is Ruddlemoor community garden. Built with the help of Imerys, this little area provides a focus for the people of the village to play and meet together. The last trains to run over the line were some chartered specials, pulled by saddle tanks based at St Blazey. The line closed in 1962 and the lines were taken up shortly after. The trackbed was left to return to nature, until it was revived as part of the clay trails system.

(G) Just a little way on, about 2 miles from St Austell, is the China Clay Country Park which marks the end of this particular clay trail. Established in the former clay dries and works of the old Wheal Martyn pits, this place is certainly a must for anyone who wants to know more about China Clay and its history. The museum is set in 26 acres of woods, hills and old buildings. They have their own publicity material and website, so details of what can be expected there are easy to find. The museum also provides one of the few places from which to observe legally and in safety the workings of the modern mining industry. At the very top of the grounds there is a viewing area where observers can look down into the huge man-made hole in the ground that is Wheal Martyn Pit. From here it is possible to watch the reality of the work involved in washing out the clay with high pressure hoses, the dumping of the overburden and some of the first stages of refining. At the museum there is a café and restaurant where much-needed refreshments are obtainable at very reasonable prices.

3289 'St Austell' was a Great Western Duke Class 4-4-0 locomotive and the last of its class, being finally withdrawn in July 1951. Designed for the mainline gradients of Devon and Cornwall it is probable that 'St Austell' visited the engine sheds at St Blazey during its lifetime.
C Edyvean

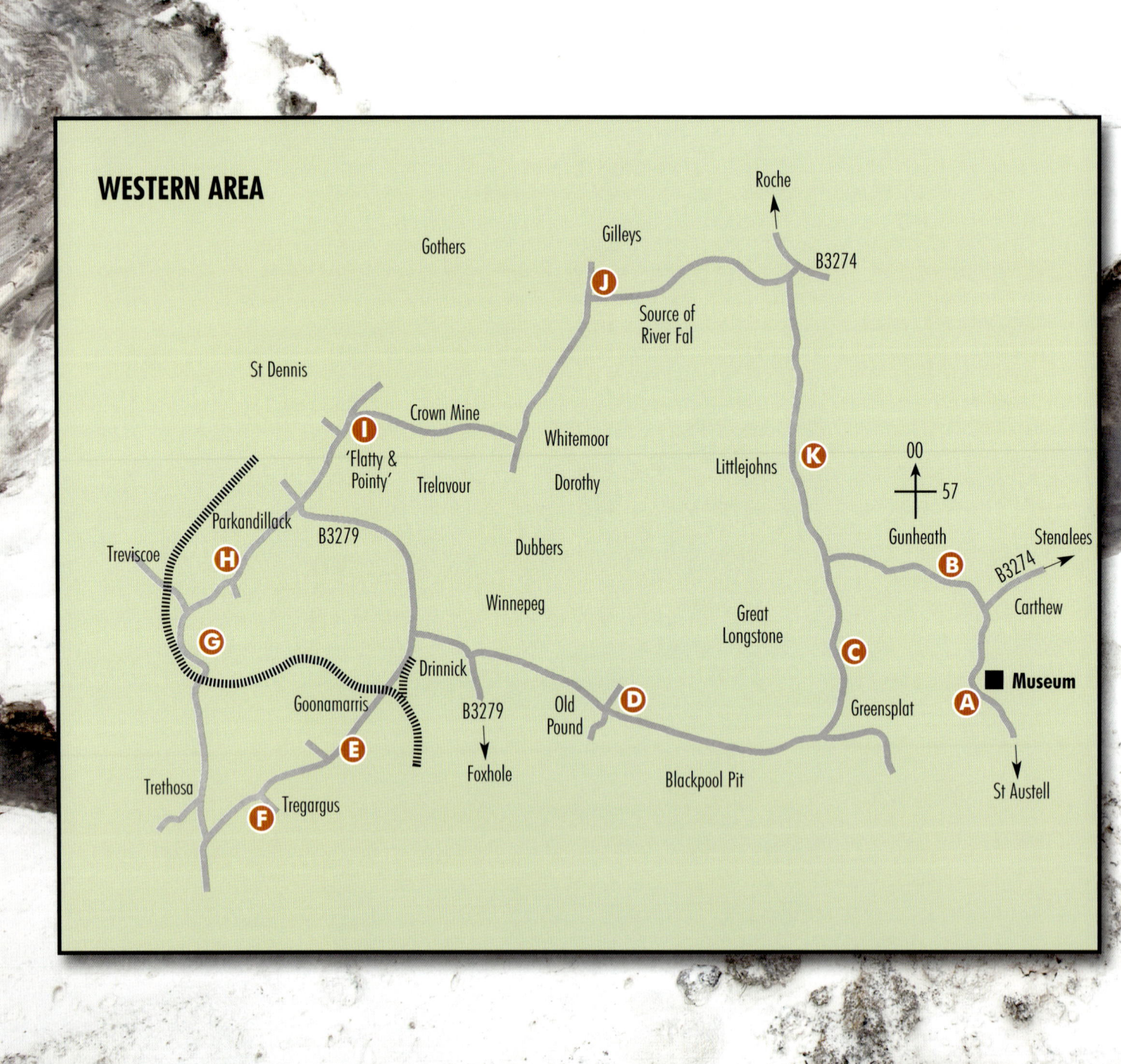

DRIVE 1 – WESTERN AREA

THOSE PEOPLE WHO ARE unable or unwilling to use the walks, yet are still curious about the area can use this suggested route to drive through some of the most important clay mining sites in mid Cornwall. There are many different ways around the district, this drive which is about ten miles long takes in much of the western area and circumnavigates the works at Great Longstone, Old Pound, Dubbers, Dorothy and Littlejohns pits. It starts and finishes at the China Clay Country Park and Museum.

(A) At the bottom of the Museum car park turn left and start up the hill in the direction of Bodmin on the B3274. At the end of the car park on the left can be seen a rather grand entrance with a lodge house. The private road only goes to some nurseries now, but its original purpose was to mark the beginning of the sweeping drive leading to the lovely old house, sadly now demolished, that belonged to Miss Ivy Martyn. A little way further on up the main road there are some older mill buildings next to the stream, one of which has a restored water wheel attached to it and which is fed by a leat taken from the infant White River. There were many water mills hereabouts, some used for processing clay, but others for the more traditional purposes of grinding corn or working industrial machinery. At this point it can be appreciated why walking along this road is not a good idea, the carriageway is narrow, hemmed in by the walls of the old schoolyard and the course of the stream.

Soon however there is a small triangular village green, so turn left here by the pub. This is the village of Carthew, another settlement developed when the mines came to the area along with the turnpike road. This hamlet marked the limit of the Carbean Branch railway line which came up from Bugle to get into Gunheath Pit. Although the two branch lines, Carbean and Lansalson came within a few hundred yards of each other they never met, the Carbean line was much higher and it would have proved difficult to engineer a connection because of the difference in height between the two tracks. The small freight line disappeared in the sixties, and very little remains of its trackbed. Carthew had its share of small businesses feeding the industry, the successors to these small operations

CORNWALL'S CHINA CLAY COUNTRY

Treviscoe China Clay Works. Adrian Brown

DRIVE 1 – WESTERN AREA

still inhabit the older buildings and although successful they often have no direct link to the Clay Industry.

(B) Climbing the hill there is a hint on the left of original woodland but that soon gives way to man made country. On the right can be seen the dark cliffs and steep slopes of Gunheath which was closed for clay production in 2002. Mechanical excavators and dumpers can be seen toiling away at the bottom and on the sides of the quarry but this is only for the production of aggregates. When it was fully working twenty-four hours a day, the sight of the cliffs lit by the floodlights was memorable. Shadows and headlights, sodium floodlights and flashing warning beacons all contrived to make the place look like a James Bond film set. The high overgrown tip standing beside Gunheath shows just how much material was capable of being transported by a simple skip and wire rope up a small inclined railway track. Just beyond the entrance to Gunheath can be seen the remains of a concrete bridge that took skips across the road to create another dump on the left.

Disused mica dam at Kernick.
Adrian Brown

CORNWALL'S CHINA CLAY COUNTRY

Above left: *Greensplat Chapel before 1929. The whole of the village was eradicated when Wheal Martyn Pit was extended in the last part of the twentieth century.*

CCHS

Above right: *Greensplat Chapel was demolished in August 2002 along with the other houses, trees, roads, telephone box and fields that made up the village. This is the last of Greensplat!*

Andrew Northam

(C) At the top of the hill turn left. Originally the road went straight ahead here across the top of Hensbarrow to Old Pound, Whitemoor and Karslake and this was a crossroads. Up a slight rise traffic lights control the passage of massive yellow dumpers as they cross the road, on their way with overburden from the depths of Wheal Martyn to be tipped high above. Just to the left, where the road starts to descend, is the site of the village of Greensplat. Here there was a chapel, several houses and a working beam engine. Under the houses there were valuable minerals, so in the first half of the twenty first century the village of Greensplat ceased to exist, obliterated by diggers, drills and explosives! Nothing except a few trees and the truncated entrance of a road now remains. The road has only recently been created to bypass the ever expanding Wheal Martyn Pit. To get a better look at the pit you can turn briefly left at the next turn and understand better the straight course of the original road that came up from St Austell through Greensplat and then on to Roche. The village straddled this road close to the water-filled pit.

Returning to the original route, the views here are extensive. St Austell Bay can be seen, the Pentewan Valley, and all the country down to the Roseland is spread out before you. This is still called the 'New Road' by some locals, indeed it is not a dedicated highway at all and could in theory be closed and dug up again for the minerals beneath it. Look at the amount of dumped material on the right and imagine what effort it took to put it there. This sand burrow is only about thirty years old and its construction is described in the Blackpool Pit chapter. The heights and depths of Blackpool appear on the left, and just over the brow of the hill is the village of Old Pound. Again there are crossroads, but the turning on the right is a dead end and leads only to Littlejohns Pit and the other mines (Longstone, Dorothy, Great Longstone, Cocksbarrow and West Gunheath) that have joined up to form the huge quarry that now occupies all this area.

(D) Keep straight ahead. Old Pound still has a small place of worship, a Bible Christian Chapel, one of the few remaining that is active and has so far resisted closure and conversion into a dwelling house. The land beyond, down the hill, is still the beating heart of the China Clay Country. Practically all the older buildings here owe their existence to the boom in the mining industry of the early part of the twentieth century. At the bottom of the hill turn right on to the B3279. In front of the T-junction are the tanks and works at Goverseth whilst the adjoining buildings and yards are all part of the Drinnick complex, referred to in another chapter. On the right are the old and new schools and a graveyard which has the distinction of being voted the best kept cemetery in the country. Just beyond Drinnick take the road left that is signed St Stephens. This leads to Goonamarris, the home of Jack Clemo who was known as the poet of the China Clay Country. His house has only recently been demolished. Clemo lived here for much of his life and his work was inspired by the landscape and people that surrounded him. Although to some his verses may seem a trifle impenetrable, he has made a lasting impression and is one of the few who has spoken of this place in terms of its culture and beauty, rather than in a disparaging fashion.

A Victorian view of Drinnick with its dryers and kilns. The green fields and essentially agricultural nature of the area are evident, not yet despoiled by the sand burrows. Trees have been felled to make way for further expansion of the pits and are piled ready for the sawbench.

CORNWALL'S CHINA CLAY COUNTRY

The internal electricity generating station at Drinnick in the 1920,s, as evidenced by the cars parked in the foreground. The wooden cooling tower eventually blew down in a gale.
CCHS

A Hy Mac swing shovel digs out the base for a tank at Goverseth works above Drinnick.
CCHS

(E) The next turning right is no longer available as a through way, boulders and sand have been heaped across it, so that it cannot be used by vehicles. The road has been closed due to a landslip failure between Slip and Goonamarris, rendering it unsafe for public use. Instead drive past the large block-making works on the left (an ideal location with as much sand as anyone might need literally on the doorstep) and down the hill. In a small layby on the left at the bottom there are some kissing gates. **(F)** A walk down through here leads to a green valley with picturesque ruins and footpaths that thread their way through the long abandoned workings of the Tregargus mills and quarries. Continue until the next turning and turn right at Hill Head or Stepaside towards Treviscoe. On the left down a side road is Trethosa Chapel which houses a small museum dedicated to the memory of Jack Clemo. In the distance can be seen some of the Fal Valley works including the Dry Mining operations area, a place that is still very much a working quarry and to which there are very few access points for the general public to observe its day to day running. This road passes between the huge redundant Kernick mica dam on the left and Trethosa and Goonvean Pits on the right. Goonvean is still expanding, and only very recently one

Tregargus Mill and the water wheel. The ruins of this complex can be accessed on foot from the St Stephens to Nanpean road.
CCHS

CORNWALL'S CHINA CLAY COUNTRY

The award winning Treviscoe Male Voice Choir that appeared at The Llangollen International Musical Eisteddfod in 1956. Choirs, bands and the like were mainly made up from people who worked in the China Clay Industry and they had huge support within their own communities.

C Edyvean

Opposite: *Spoil dumping has always been a part of clay mining, with the iconic white pyramids being a reminder of the history of the process. In recent times the spoil is carried in huge vehicles as seen in this photograph.*

Adrian Brown

of the last working beam engines was removed to be taken to a museum. The building which housed it was then summarily demolished to get at the clay underneath. Trethosa Pit no longer works and is being backfilled.

(G) Just after the railway bridge there are close up views of some small settling tanks and Treviscoe Dryers. Not everything produced here goes by rail and signs in German and Dutch for the lorries that are loaded bear testament to the European-wide trade that is carried on. Just before the village of Treviscoe itself turn right heading towards St Dennis. If you go through Treviscoe you can see the chapel which was the home of one of the most famous of the local choirs. Treviscoe Male Voice Choir, which under its conductor Russell Kessell, won the Welsh International Eisteddfod in 1956, a glorious achievement that is still remembered with great pride to this day.

(H) The big works on the left are Parkandillack. They are the highest point that the railway presently reaches, although there is talk about reopening the mile or so of still existing track bed which would rejoin it to the main Newquay to Par Branch line at Fraddon. This is the place where currently there are proposals to build an incinerator to take much of Cornwall's domestic refuse. Many local people are against such plans, a public enquiry is at present underway to determine the outcomes of the strategy for waste management here and within the county as a whole. Parkandillack houses one of the few complete beam engine houses in

DRIVE 1 – WESTERN AREA

CORNWALL'S CHINA
CLAY COUNTRY

Parkandillack 30' Engine House with round settling tanks and button-hole launders. This remains the only complete beam engine still in working condition in the area.
CCHS

A rail tour, The 'China Clay Pony', headed by Black Five 76079 in May 2006 goes as far as it can. Just a hundred yards beyond this point at Parkandillack Refineries the line to Fraddon has been lifted, although the track bed is intact and there is talk of reopening this stretch to make an alternative route into Newquay.
R. Fogg

DRIVE 1 – WESTERN AREA

Perched on the edge of the pit, the Goonvean Engine House, standing in the way of further excavation work, had to be removed. The Cornish draught pumping engine, which had stopped work in 1956, together with its beam was taken out in September 2008 and after cleaning and repair will go on display at Harveys Foundry Trust in Hayle.

R. Fogg

In the autumn of 2010 the Goonvean Engine House was finally demolished and the work of excavating the surrounding area could carry on. Soon there will be no trace of where the Engine had stood since 1910.

R. Fogg

the area. It no longer runs on steam, compressed air is used to drive the engine and move the beam up and down. It is looked after by a group of volunteers who sometimes open it to the public. All the land below the road belongs to the Goonvean China Clay Company and Imerys so the public cannot drive down there without permission. At the next junction, drive across the main B3279 road and go up past the fire station. St Dennis is on the left, with the nature reserve at Goss Moor stretching out beyond, and the main A30 cutting through it. The church stands high on a hill close to the village.

Many of the houses in St Dennis are of the Cornish Unit type, a common design used for council housing in the fifties and sixties. The distinctive double apex mansard style roof makes these buildings instantly recognisable all over the country. In fact they were nearly all designed and built in Cornwall by ECLP, just a mile or so from St Dennis at Gothers. Initially designed to provide quick and cheap low-cost post war housing, the pre-formed concrete panels from which they were made slotted together to make excellent family

CORNWALL'S CHINA CLAY COUNTRY

Loading the mainline wagons before the war was heavy manual work. Here wagons belonging to ECLP can be seen in a siding at Quarry Close near Foxhole.
CCHS

homes. Originally the project was kick-started by the use of German prisoners of war employed as cheap labour together with abundant supplies of raw material. Selleck, Nicholls, Williams (SNW), was the name of the construction side of ECC and were the people behind the development of Cornish Units.

Looking back more of the Fal Valley workings can be seen in the distance and Trelavour Downs, covered in another chapter, is on the right. **(I)** Turn right towards Whitemoor and pass 'Pointy and Flatty' the two sky tips on the right. In Whitemoor village, just after the school turn left and head towards Roche. On the right is the Dorothy Pit entrance, now locked, which marked the start of the old road to Greensplat. With another landscaped burrow on the right, descend Cleers Hill, and turn right opposite Allens Tyres, the sign says 'Stenalees'. This is another 'New Road', again built to replace older, now buried highways. Close to this road is what is generally accepted as the source of the River Fal, hidden in the fields beneath the burrows. **(J)** The disused mica dam at Gilleys can be clearly seen, as can the village church at Roche. Gilleys is now fully restored to heathland with a network of footpaths and bridleways across it and can be used in conjunction with the adjacent Goss Moor trails.

Just before this 'New Road' meets the main B3274 road at a T-junction close to a big car dismantling yard, turn right up the hill through moorland towards Greensplat once more. **(K)** This hill goes up to what was once the highest point in the area, and at the top there is a small car park on the left just before the haul road crossing and close to the high telecommunications mast. This mast is a feature which can be seen from many miles away, less so the smaller barrow at Hensbarrow on which is perched a trig point and which marked the highest point of the range of hills at a height of 312 metres. This is now completely dwarfed by the reseeded sand burrows which tower over the old marker and reach a height of 355 metres. It is possible to walk from the car park across to the beacon, and indeed wander about on the heathland following the footpath signs.

Out of the car park and continue left, the whole of St Austell Bay comes into view. It is at this point that both coasts can be easily seen on a fine day. There are remains of small farms, fields and cottages, most of which have been demolished. In a few places the land is still worked so it is possible to imagine the network of agricultural settlements that once prospered up here. Surprisingly there is a small wood of mature trees nestling in a hollow and trying bravely to hang on to life despite the wind and mining activities that surround them. This road bears left and starts downhill back to Carthew. Drift down Gunheath Hill, turn right on the main road and back to the museum where the drive started.

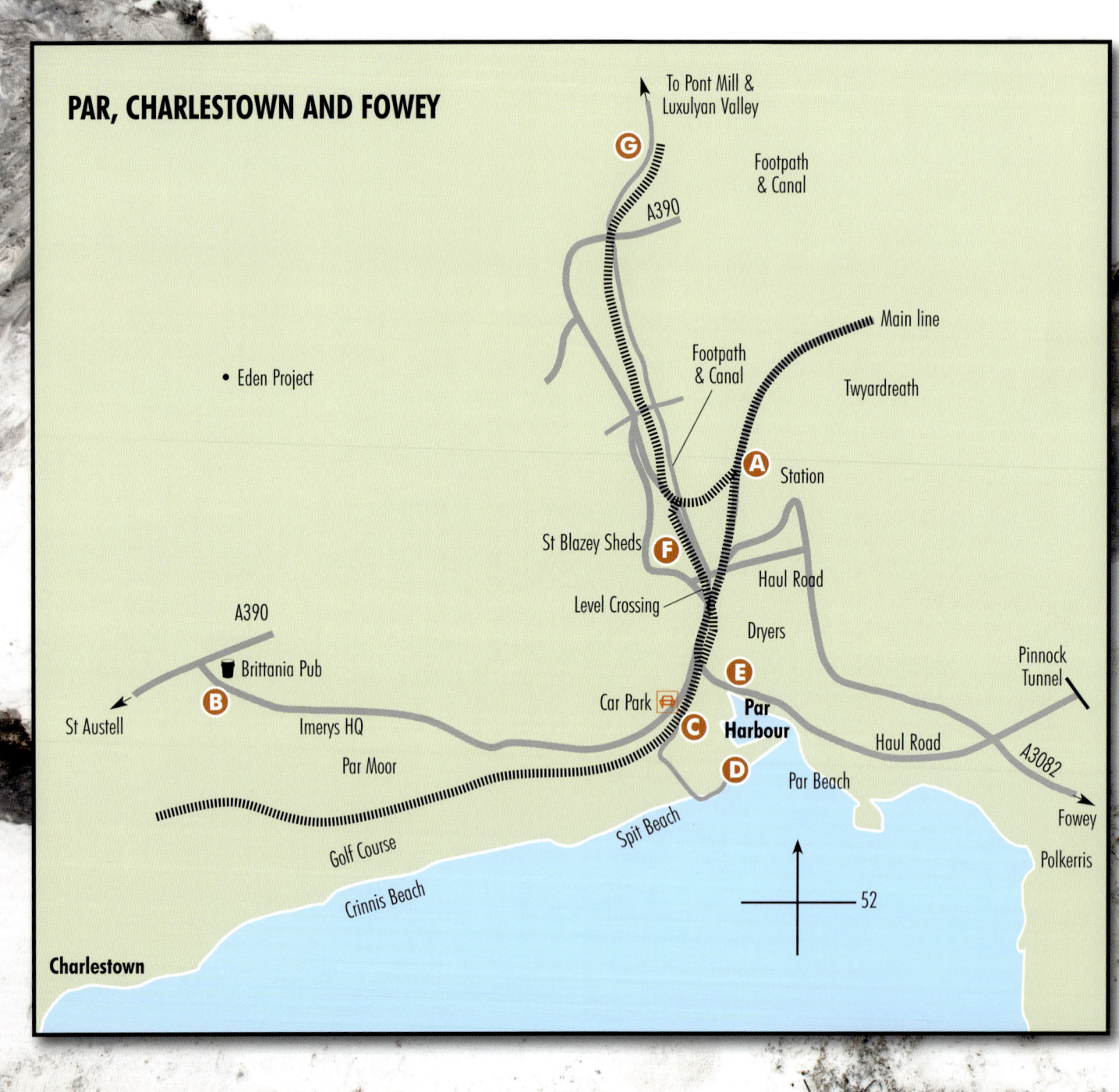

THE PORTS OF PAR, CHARLESTOWN AND FOWEY

THIS CHAPTER IS DESIGNED to give some understanding of the history of the ports and their immediate environment but does not allow for walking tours as do the other guides in this book. Par and Fowey can only be viewed from a distance; the main reason for this is the lack of public access. Par Harbour is a working area despite being closed to clay shipping and it is still being developed, whilst Fowey is even harder to see except by river. Charlestown is open and functions as a tourist village with many attractions and parking places. Although they have much in common, each port will be described separately.

Charlestown Harbour.
Adrian Brown

CORNWALL'S CHINA CLAY COUNTRY

The heavy wide-wheeled wagons of clay that had come down from the hills were unloaded directly into the holds of ships in Charlestown harbour. The wooden shutes that were also used can be seen in the background.

C Edyvean

Because most of the customers for the china clay were in distant parts of Britain and Europe an effective means of transport had to be developed to get it out of Cornwall. To a certain degree the advent of an integrated road and rail system provided for this, but still the transport of the heavy china clay in large amounts could most easily be done by sea. Although some of the ports on the north coast such as Newquay, Wadebridge, and Padstow together with the Channel ports of Falmouth and Plymouth were used in the early years, the nearest harbour of any significance to the clay mines was Fowey. This was still some miles away, so it was that in early Victorian times three local entrepreneurial families took it upon themselves to create new ports to service the burgeoning industry. The Hawkins family built Pentewan, the Rashleighs built Charlestown and the Treffrys created Par. In the hinterland behind Charlestown and Par there developed a large number of related industries, houses, roads, railways and other industrial activities..

Charlestown, the port nearest to St Austell is now a big tourist attraction, offering close up views of, and even voyages on, authentic Square Riggers. It has a vibrant summertime café and pub scene, there is a big Shipwreck and Heritage Museum housed in one of the former clay buildings, and it has been used by many film companies as a location for their productions. This is a far cry from its original purpose which was to ship the clay out using a dock that had gates which could be closed in order to maintain the water levels at

The Oranus is inside the dock at Charlestown and is being loaded using the shutes. Lorries, in this case ex-army Bedfords, tip their clay from high above the ship creating clouds of white dust that spreads over harbour, houses, ships and people.

C Edyvean

Charlestown Engineering. This is the foundry in 1987 and molten cast iron is being poured into a mould. Not many years later the whole place was closed and demolished.

CCHS

all times. In truth it has no natural reason to be here. Before it was built by the Rashleigh family there was just a small inlet at Polmear Cove where a stream flowed into the bay and small luggers would be beached in order to load them before the tide came back in again. What you see today is completely man made, built by Victorian and late eighteenth century engineers and backed up by an infrastructure that included a leat which ran from Luxulyan four miles away to top up the water in the dock. As the port developed the population of the village grew, and it became much busier. Unfortunately the dock was only designed for small sailing ships, and cargo vessels were getting much larger. Inevitably there came a time when the last commercial shipment of clay left Charlestown. In fact this only happened as recently as 2000.

Small coasters would enter Charlestown cautiously on a high tide. The many intrigued onlookers would note how shouted instructions and radio were used together, crewmen would stand on the ship while on the dockside, watching and giving orders, would be the Harbourmaster. Ropes were used to aid the manoeuvres as the ship was turned and squeezed through the open lock gates. Finally as the boat was brought alongside, the gates would be shut. Whilst the tide fell the still floating ship would begin to be loaded. In the latter years the cargo of clay only came from one of the smaller clay companies. Their lorries would come down over the hill to the little weighbridge and be checked in. The drivers would then have to reverse along the top of the high wall above the moored ships, loosen the tarpaulin covering the powdered clay then tip the load down chutes straight into the open hold. Great clouds of dust always accompanied this action after which the empty lorry would make way for another as the process was repeated until the vessel was fully loaded. Only then would the ship be let out of the dock in reverse, on the next suitable tide.

Amongst the many dries, linhays, fish cellars, lime kilns and other buildings associated with this little working port was an engineering company. Known as Charlestown Engineering it was founded in 1823 and was one of the few heavy industrial works that existed in this part of Cornwall. They produced mining machinery and latterly designed and built much of the specialised equipment for use in the clay mining industry. Even today there are still a few places that use pumps made by Charlestown Engineering. With the decline in the industry it changed hands several times before finally closing in 2004, to be demolished and replaced by a housing estate. Generations of skilled and inventive workers had produced high quality products from this site, and sent them all over the world. The workers at Charlestown Engineering became redundant or found what other work they could. Now, as in so many cases, engineering work is contracted out and the machines used to mine the clay come from other places The decline of the works was felt by many, not the least by one of the Engineering Managers who kept his small traction engine at the foundry. He was most indignant when asked to remove it and find a new home for his pride and joy.

(A) Par Harbour can be seen from the train window as it pulls up the steep gradient away from Par Station bound for St Austell; the view is the only real glimpse of the sea between Saltash and Penzance. Its all pervading white buildings and steaming chimneys were once a familiar and comforting sight to many Cornish people as they returned home, there was only one place like this in the world! Par Harbour was built between 1830 and 1836 by Thomas Treffry who was by then at the height of his powers He needed to not only get the metal ore away from the many mines that he owned, but also to service the growing china clay trade

THE PORTS OF PAR, CHARLESTOWN AND FOWEY

Par Docks. Adrian Brown

CORNWALL'S CHINA CLAY
COUNTRY

Par Docks. Adrian Brown

Great Treverbyn Mill in 1945, one of the dries on Par Moor road. The lorries belong to W & G Hawke of Polgooth, named people include Garfield Northcott, Hart Roach, Audrey Bond, Barbara Beard, Olive Hughes and a man named Brokenshire.

CCHS

Heavy Transport Lorry Park in 1969. The ground is compacted sand, later this was concreted over. The lorries are mostly Commers with their unusual two-stroke diesel engines, but some Fords are just visible.

CCHS

and bring in the coal, timber and other materials to keep his empire running smoothly. Other books go into much more detail about Treffry's empire, and can be consulted, but briefly the provision of his harbour formed an important link in the progress of the china clay from his quarries via the roads, canals, and railways which he had built, on to the barges and ships that were tied alongside the jetties or anchored out in the bay.

(B) In fact the road between Par Harbour and its junction with the A390 at the Britannia Inn, known as Par Moor, has more than a passing significance for the clay industry. Opposite Par Market is a large business park, and this was the home of The Heavy Transport Company Ltd. 'Heavy Transport' was the base for all the large blue and white trucks that were once such a familiar sight around the area. A lot of clay was moved around the district by road following the deregulation of the road transport industry and huge specialised trucks and tankers hauled loads from the clay dries and then onwards to the Midlands and the North using the motorways. Nearly all the clay is now moved by rail, so the large fleet of HGVs has all but disappeared. Most of the vehicles used today are either contracted in or are confined to the pits and not allowed on the public roads. Close to the entrance of the business park is an older building with a wonderful art deco sign on it, advertising the fact that this space was also used by Selleck Nicholls, another division of the clay industry which played its part as a haulage contractor as well as a major housebuilder.

Further along Par Moor in the direction of Par is the headquarters of Imerys. These are the offices built for the French firm which took over from ECC, and who relocated there from the impressive John Keay House which had been built in the mid sixties as the worldwide HQ of English China Clays Ltd. John Keay House is now the home of Cornwall College.

To get an up-to-date look at Par Harbour is not too easy at the time of writing as about half of the site has been closed and the rest is off limits to the public. Several factors have contributed to this abandonment by the clay boats; the fact that the harbour is not deep enough to allow large ocean going vessels to anchor (older ships could happily rest on the bottom when the tide went out), and also the general downturn in the clay industry mean that all the sea going cargoes now go out from Fowey. The whole western part of the complex is awaiting reconstruction or demolition. There is a general air of neglect, bushes grow from old settling tanks, seagulls nest on grass covered roofs and railway tracks are concreted over.

Below left: *Ford Jekta Lorry known as 'The Old Bath' unloading into a ships hold at Par Docks in june 1951.*
CCHS

Below right: *The Jeckta had an unusual telescopic butt operated by a hydraulic ram which can be seen in action here. This seems to have been an experimental version; few other examples of this method of unloading are known to have been adopted.*
CCHS

CORNWALL'S CHINA CLAY COUNTRY

Par Harbour, and a Euclid TS14 Motor Scraper and Dozer driven by Gerald Mitchell are clearing the entrance channel on a low tide.
CCHS

This turn of the century postcard shows the original layout of Treffrys harbour at Par. Beyond can just be made out the small village of Polkerris.
C Edyvean

(C) For a better view, park in the small unnamed car park on the St Austell side of the new railway bridge just outside the main entrance to the harbour. This is the entrance to Spit beach, although there are no signs to that effect. The path goes beneath a very low bridge which carries the main railway line. The minimal height restriction here is the reason why two of the preserved tank engines, now steamed regularly at the Bodmin and Wenford Railway and which worked only within Par Harbour were so low. They were designed specifically to pass under this bridge. The tracks have long since disappeared but there were sidings all along the main road serving the now derelict linhays or clay stores housing the kaolin that awaited shipping. The remains of these buildings can be seen hidden in the bushes all around.

(D) Walk under the low bridge and turn right, the coast path is dark and unkempt but well used. Passing over a pedestrian bridge between the prestigious Carlyon Bay Golf Course and the redundant buildings of the harbour the path emerges directly on to the sands and rocks of Spit Beach. This is St Austell Bay, with Charlestown half a mile or so west and Fowey just around the headland out of sight. Across the bay is Polkerris and beyond is Gribbin Head with its daymark tower. Kilmarth, the one time home of Daphne

THE PORTS OF PAR, CHARLESTOWN AND FOWEY

Sea thrift, Par harbour. Adrian Brown

CORNWALL'S CHINA CLAY COUNTRY

A rake of empty wagons has just come down from Fowey, through Pinnock Tunnel and along the back of Par Beach on its way to the marshalling yards at St Blazey. This branch line is now the privately owned haul road used exclusively by clay traffic.
C Edyvean

Above left: Although motor vessels dominate there are still examples of sailing ships to be found alongside the quay in Par Harbour. Note the ex WD Bedford OY lorry being loaded with coal in the early fifties.
CCHS

Above right: Par Harbour in the early fifties with the little saddle tank 'Judy' puffing along the water's edge. This locomotive is now on display in a preserved and running state at the Bodmin and Wenford Steam Railway.
CCHS

du Maurier sits in the trees above Polkerris, she was often to be seen striding across the fields or driving her little DAF car down to Par beach to exercise her dogs. Walk left along the beach and the harbour wall with its massive stone blocks which protects the harbour from the Southerly Gales can be seen. Beyond, the ground is private and you are only supposed to go there if you have a fishing permit, but even so from the beach you can get an idea of the layout of the wharves and jetties. Thirty or forty years ago a small flotilla of coasters could be seen anchored just outside the harbour, awaiting the tides and a berth. Sticking out from the sea a pole marks the Killyvarder rocks and the start of the dredged channel leading to the harbour entrance. Because ECC were able to use their own heavy plant on the beach, big bulldozers and scrapes were used on the low tide to supplement the work of floating dredgers. Ships have still been known to run aground here, and there are photographs of fully laden ships with most of their cargo dumped on to the beach in order to refloat them on the high water.

This half of the harbour is due to be redeveloped as part of the new Eco Town idea. There are plans to turn all this into a marina with associated housing and commercial developments. Although some may question how marinas can be ecologically friendly, the company will fully consult with locals to ensure eco-status. It is not difficult to see how appealing this site is to a developer however, and the general air of dereliction, the muddy beach and tumble down walls all show how neglected this area has become. Gone are the days when the jetties were full of cranes, puffing steam engines shunting wagon loads of clay, conveyor belts and the air of a genuine sea port. The characters that once worked here included one gentleman who doubled out of shift as an undertaker. He was also an ace motorcyclist and would invite unsuspecting visitors to have a look at the sights from the comfort of his sidecar. He would then tip the outfit on to its side and still doing some thirty miles an hour aviate the third wheel and terrified passenger right out over the side of the jetty as he nonchalantly gave them a commentary on the ships tied up alongside.

5051 'Earl Bathurst' a visiting 4-6-0 Castle Class locomotive on a special train has just come off the turntable at St Blazey. The engine sheds behind are preserved, the turntable is the only one left in Cornwall.
R. Fogg

(E) On the other side of the harbour all is different. After going under the low bridge back by the car park and turning left along the coast path, pass by the main entrance of the harbour. At present entry into the docks is illegal. Look beyond the abandoned Seaman's Mission and offices, past the defunct café and stores and a more vibrant and ultra modern picture emerges. The clay is still dried here but using the latest processes which link pits and refiners to dryers, filter presses, and calciners Steam still issues from chimneys and white dust is evident, but in much smaller quantities than previously due to the tightening up of environmental rules. From these buildings the clay is taken by lorry to Fowey for onward shipping by the clever use of an abandoned railway track which has been converted to a haul road for company use only. This is the old branch line from St Blazey to Fowey and passes behind Par Beach and onwards through Pinnock Tunnel, emerging just inland from the wharves at Fowey. In this way there is no clay traffic on the steep and narrow main public road which goes over the hill and into the heart of the old town.

Pinnock Tunnel between Par and Fowey on the former branch line is now used exclusively by the clay industry for its clay lorries.
R. Fogg

(F) St Blazey was a railway town, and the large marshalling yards, sheds, and wagon repair shops which grew up were a main source of employment for the town. Many of the men worked day and night to keep the trains running in all kinds of weathers and conditions. Here the trains with their open and hooded wagons were assembled for the daily workings of full and empties to and from the ports and the mines. Access to the docks from the marshalling yard was alongside the road, under the five-arched bridge. When the diesels came, most of the railwaymen were glad to see the back of the steam locomotives. There was a lot of railway traffic here at one stage and the level crossing gates were in constant use, now however there is little if any movement over these lines.

CORNWALL'S CHINA CLAY COUNTRY

Fowey in 1903 was still very much a working harbour where tall ships could come and go without too many problems. Although it was a long way from the mines there was even then a considerable trade in china clay. This postcard shows an early view of the harbour looking out to sea.

C Edyvean

The railway still has a presence here although it is nothing like it once was. If you want to have a closer look then the footpath between the level crossing and the caravan site which runs alongside Treffry's canal allows views, (better in the winter when the trees have lost their leaves) of the round house with its turntable and radial sidings. These buildings once housed the locomotives which were used extensively on the branch lines and marshalling yards although 'Judy' and 'Alfred' the two little Bagnall saddle tanks owned by ECC had their own small sheds actually on the harbour itself. The Round Houses are now used as industrial units but are listed and cannot be knocked down. This turntable is the last one left in Cornwall and is still used when large mainline steam engines come into the County. They are reversed up from Penzance and put on the turntable to point them in the right direction, even though it means that they still have to be driven backwards all the way to Penzance again. This is a good place to get up close to the big locomotives because they sometimes get shedded here for a few days whilst they are serviced and coaled up ready for the journey back up country. You can also use the pedestrian crossing over the lines next to the iron bridge used by the Par to Newquay trains to go over the river and canal. **(G)** This footpath follows the canal and railway through Par and will eventually end up at Ponts Mill which is part of the Saints Way and leads to the picturesque waterwheel and viaduct in the Luxulyan Valley.

Fowey has always been one of the main ports for the export of china clay, its main advantage being that it can accommodate large ocean going ships, and the docks and wharves are not greatly affected by the state of the tide. There are some extremely large ships which come in here and turn around in the dredged river by Mixtow. The whole area has historically been inaccessible by road but the railway has always managed to bring the clay in from the mines. Once the harbour was served by the Par and St Blazey line, with heavily laden trains struggling uphill through the long and smoky Pinnock Tunnel to bring their loads alongside the jetties. Now that this line is closed and used as

The wagon tip at Fowey no 8 jetty in 1910. CCHS

CORNWALL'S CHINA CLAY COUNTRY

Two views showing the loading china clay at Fowey Docks.
Adrian Brown

a road, all rail traffic goes via Lostwithiel, following the winding River Fowey through Golant and the steeply wooded valley to the end point. In former years loaded wagons would be tipped up on their end and the cargo of clay would slide out to be caught below and put on conveyors straight into the ships holds. The wagons would then be moved onwards to an adjacent track and returned empty to Lostwithiel or St Blazey where they were kept prior to going on to works such as Burngullow where they could be loaded straight from the clay dry. Nowadays there are more sophisticated systems using conveyors and integrated specialist railway wagons. Fowey station was closed in the early sixties, and access to the working areas around the wharves is strictly denied to the public for obvious reasons.

The wharves here are modern, the storage facilities large, and the equipment massive. This is a truly industrial process which is carried out in the most tranquil of settings. The trees may be still be covered in some white dust, and the river which was the setting for Wind in the Willows may not look as if can sustain this kind of activity, but in fact there is something quite romantic about the prospects of ships as large as these still visiting this ancient port. John Masefield with his 'Dirty British coaster with its salt caked smokestack' would have immediately recognised the scene, even though very few of the visiting ships are British registered.

Some years ago a pair of small coasters were anchored side by side in the river awaiting loading. A passing canoeist whose curiosity had got the better of him paddled between the two for a closer inspection. Having successfully passed between the two steel walls of the ships he was moving away from the vessels when he heard a clang. Turning round he was slightly perturbed to see that the two hulls had come together and not even the smallest piece of driftwood would fit between them.

Soon after the Berlin Wall fell many Eastern European ships came into the port, and parked in odd corners on the jetties could be found groups of old Lada cars. Ladas were regarded as excellent vehicles in the Baltic Ports, and the long tradition of the sea captain as entrepreneur meant that a subsidiary trade as deck cargo flourished, albeit briefly. The best way to look at the modern port of Fowey is to hire a boat from the many available in the old harbour, perhaps you can see things happening if you take the Bodinnick Ferry, and there is a footpath from Bodinnick to Mixtow. However, don't try to get into the docks by foot, they are definitely off limits!

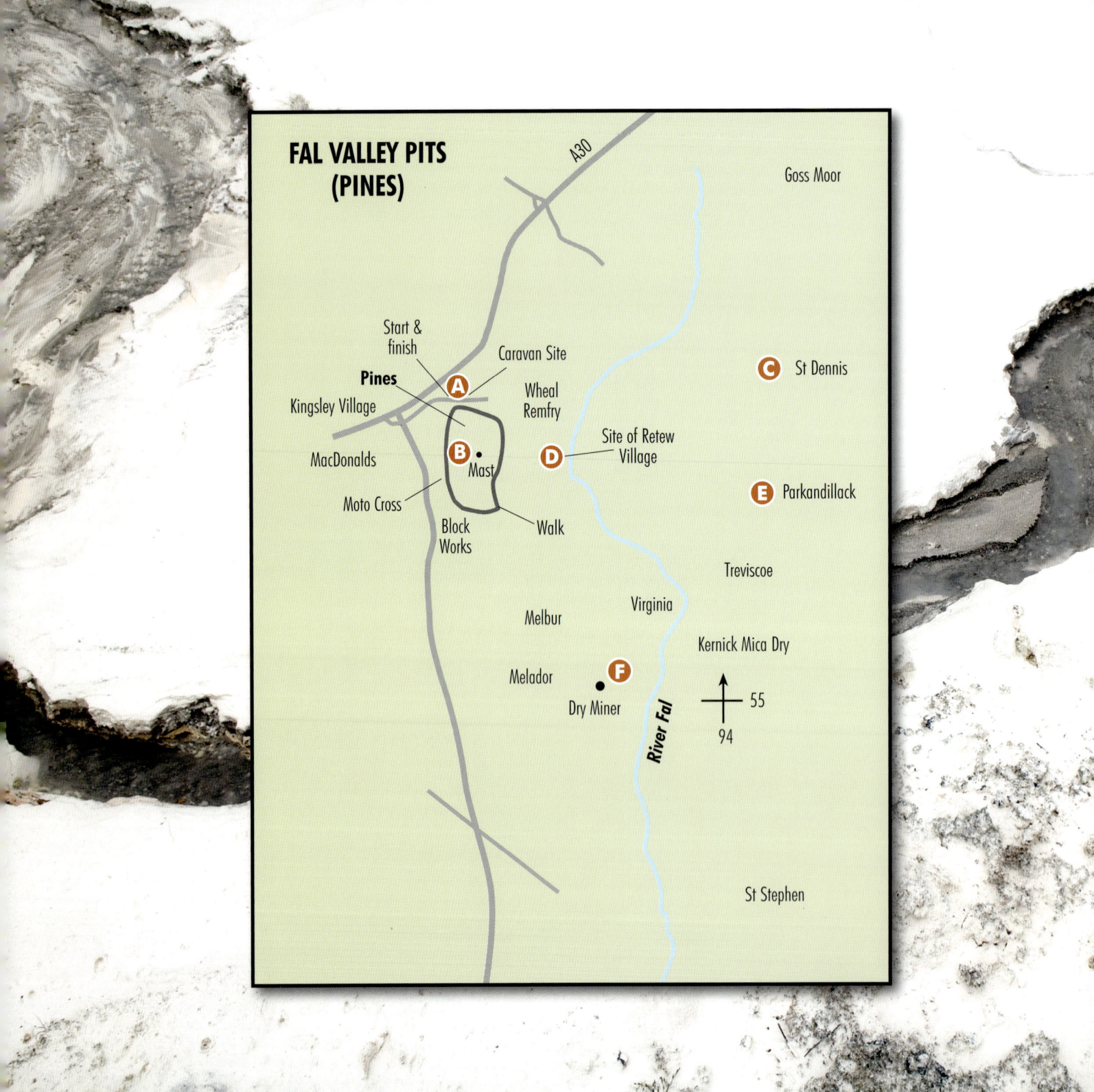

FAL VALLEY PITS

PINES TIP IS ONE of the few places from which to view a working pit in safety, and it also provides magnificent views across the county which contrast the farming communities of mid Cornwall with those of the adjacent china clay mining area. The start of this short walk is very close to Kingsley Village on the main A30 at Fraddon, a place known locally as Hamburger Hill. There are no toilets, and there is one steep path, but the rest of the track is easily passable and it's only about a mile in length. To get to the start by car, leave the Jet petrol station next to Macdonalds, turn right and go beneath the main A30 dual carriageway. Almost immediately turn left up a minor road that is signposted to Retew.

Melbur refinery, the 'Dry Miner'.

Adrian Brown

CORNWALL'S CHINA CLAY COUNTRY

Melbur China Clay Works. Adrian Brown

(A) Just where the hill begins to flatten out, opposite two gateways there is a kissing gate on the right and the start of the track. There is plenty of room to park, just keep to the verges and don't block the gateways.

Go through the gate and keep the trees on the right. There is clear evidence of a track which rises sharply to the left, ignore this and keep on the main path which descends gradually until it is barred by a gate. Although the gate can be opened, and the track follows the base of the hill, the narrow and steep uphill path to the left is the one to follow. As it rises sharply and unevenly, the view over the countryside begins to open up. After a few zig zags this path emerges at the top of the plateau, through a gate in the fence. There is a wooden bench here and the view is spectacular. On a good day the high ground to the west of St Ives can be seen, as can Kit Hill near the River Tamar; a distance of 35 to 40 miles.

Immediately below are the sandplant and blockworks at Melbur which use sand and gravel straight from the pit to produce the building materials which are so much a part of the local architecture. In Cornwall the use of traditional building bricks is much less common than are the breeze blocks which have been manufactured from cheap and readily obtainable clay waste. Next to the blockworks is a recently constructed moto cross circuit, ideally located here close to the main road yet far enough away from houses such

Melbur Mill near the lower end of the Retew branch line in the early sixties. Much of the field system behind the buildings has disappeared and the 'Dry Miner' now stands about where the more distant chimney is. The River Fal in the foreground was very badly treated at the time, it now runs clean and pollution free.

CCHS

CORNWALL'S CHINA CLAY COUNTRY

Melbur Pit.
Adrian Brown

108

CORNWALL'S CHINA CLAY COUNTRY

Melbur in the 1930s, emptying the mica drags. The slow running water in the drags would separate out the sand from the clay rich mixture. The fluid would then have to be channelled into tanks for further settlement to occur whilst the remaining unwanted sand would be taken off to the tip.
CCHS

Lampered! (covered in muck). Melbur No 4 Dry and filter press cakes are wheeled out. The cakes were the result of clay being dried by loading it into a high pressure press and squeezing as much water as possible out of it. The hard job was to drop the presses, that is to say to retrieve the solid cakes of clay from the frames often by manually levering them apart.
CCHS

that noise and traffic is not a problem. Looking south and west the Ladock valley can be traced as it makes its way from the Goss Moor south towards Truro, and beyond that the lush farmland stretches out towards the Roseland Peninsula. Follow the main A30 as it passes through Fraddon, Summercourt and Mitchell towards the windmills at Carland Cross. In the distance are St Agnes Beacon, Carn Brea, The Lizard, Falmouth and Gerrans Bay. The sea at Newquay glints in the sunlight and aircraft arriving at Newquay Airport can be watched as they lower their wheels and come into land on the runway adjacent to the wood.

(B) Its good to spend a while just sitting on this bench and absorbing the atmosphere; this is truly a beautiful county and the woods and fields, houses and villages, valleys and hills are essential elements in the mix which makes this place something rather special.

110

However much the observer may wish to linger, the point of the walk is to look at China Clay Country, so pass through the gate and follow the path keeping the fence on the right. The whole of this plateau is made up ground, created by legions of dumpers and excavators moving overburden from the pits below. This is called Pines Tip because a group of trees which once grew here were all buried during these operations. With the newly planted trees on the slopes and the flat top retained as heath land it is almost a place where Conan Doyle's 'Lost World' might be found where instead of giant lizards roaming and pterodactyls flying there are rabbits and skylarks. Continue along the track for just a few hundred yard until it turns back on itself and presents another, quite different but equally spectacular face of Cornwall. The opportunity to look down into a working china clay pit from a place of safety is rare. Dominating the whole panorama are the sand burrows, the sky tips and pits, the villages that grew up around the industry and the buildings put in place to support the industrial processes. The contrast with the view to the south could not be greater, yet this is what mid Cornwall has been about for nearly 200 years.

Throughout the landscape, although often hidden from sight, runs the River Fal. It rises in the uplands of the Goss Moor and makes its way to the sea through St Stephen, Grampound and eventually Tregony and the creeks on the Roseland Peninsula. Meanwhile on the western side of Pines the Tresillian River flows down the Ladock Valley and eventually joins up with the Fal down near the King Harry Ferry. The Fal carved out the wooded valley below with its steeply sloping sides and passed through the gaps in the granite hills. Here the miners started to produce raw materials from not only decayed kaolin but also from the tin, iron and other mineral deposits that occurred hereabouts. It's very easy to see the layout of the Victorian landscape at a time before all the tips and pits were fully established. The lands between the railway and ports of the south coast and the quarries in central Cornwall where the minerals were mined rose to a great height. Imagine how much easier it would have been to go around rather than over the hills or to carefully pick a way down the valley following the bank of the river. **(C)** The village Church at St Dennis stands prominently on a hill surrounded by ancient medieval field systems with their impressive granite walls and hedges. The development of the roads and railways can be traced; the railway line to Parkandillack and the disused track bed following the Fal down to Melbur close to the village of St Stephens can be made out. There are distant views of the Newquay branch line and the modern A30 as it cuts its way down from Roche across the Goss Moor.

The network of much smaller roads linking the older villages, fields, farms and towns can be seen, as can the sea on both coasts. Although clay from Bodmin Moor was shipped out

CORNWALL'S CHINA CLAY COUNTRY

Wheal Remfry brickworks derelict, showing the remains of the beehive kiln. It was closed in 1977.
CCHS

Wheal Remfry no 4 in 1978, a dumper pulling a load of polyurethane pipes for a residue line which was being constructed.
CCHS

of Newquay, Padstow and other north coast ports, the south coast was the one with the most accessible harbours, the calmest seas and the best transport connections. This was the direction that the wagons of china clay were sent on their way out of Cornwall, and this remains so to this day although modern road transport still accesses the A30 as the main spine road out of the County. To understand and interpret the comings and goings within the valley needs a bit of time and patience, but pretty much the whole of the washing and de watering process can be observed from up here, although the refining is done at Melbur just down the valley and out of view.

The valley was once a series of much smaller pits, pumping stations, tank sites and dryers. Now they have been subsumed into one huge operation although their names linger on as working areas within the complex; Wheal Remfry, Melbur and Virginia are all examples of this. **(D)** If you look carefully down beside the old dry you might see a couple of monkey puzzle trees standing high above the native oaks and sycamores. This is a part of the complex known as 'The Square'. It is so called because it was once exactly that, the centre of a village called Retew. This village, like many others has been totally obliterated by the expansion of mining operations. It was once a fair sized community with its own chapel and mill. Gradually the quarries crept closer and the little cob cottages were overwhelmed or demolished. The people moved out and now all that remains are memories and a few ancient trees. **(E)** The way that led to the village can still be seen although it is not accessible to the public; follow the old track from the Treviscoe road on the opposite side of the valley, down past the disused South Fraddon Dry with the chimney at one end, to what was once the village centre, then imagine it coming up the side of the cliffs and joining the road very close to the mobile home site near the start of this walk.

Another of Richards and Sharps' Peerless wagons from just after the First World War doing sterling work hauling clay.
CCHS

Looking down it's not easy to sort things out, so let's start at the highest point, just below the footpath. This is the outer edge of the mine and consists of steep slopes, cliff faces and innumerable tracks. Along various levels, or benches to give them their proper name, an observer may be able to see some small cabins or huts. These huts house the controls that the operator, known as the 'Hoseman' uses to direct the jet of high pressure water towards the mix of clay, rock, sand and mica in front of him. The material may have been blasted by explosives from the side of the pit, then pushed up into a stope, or cliff face, by a huge bulldozer. This is a continuous process; you may be lucky enough to see this in action. When washing the clay from the stope, the hoseman will often work in conjunction with a large mechanical loading shovel which removes most of the unwanted stone whilst the clay starts its journey to the pit bottom. The rock mixture is given the name 'stent' and is

Monitor at work.

Adrian Brown

placed in a nearby stockpile. By far the largest proportion of the stockpile is then moved to one of the huge stent tips that surround the Fal Valley area although some will be diverted for use in the sand and blockworks at Melbur on the other side of Pines. The stent or overburden is the waste; it constitutes 50% of all mined material and poses a major headache in its disposal. It is what Pines, where you are standing, is made of.

The wide tracks on the levels look smooth, but a Land Rover is really the best vehicle to get around in: there are very deep ruts, large boulders and glutinous patches of white

FAL VALLEY PITS

The high-pressure hose known as the monitor washing clay away from the stent or unwanted rock. The manually controlled old-fashioned versions were hard work, in winter the spray would freeze and it was not uncommon for the hoseman to be completely covered in an icy coating. Now they are remotely operated from a heated cabin some distance away from the actual jet of water.

CCHS

Clearing sand from the gravel pump in a sink. The pit bottom man's job was to make sure that the pump did not get 'buried up'.

CCHS

mud that can easily stop ordinary vehicles and indeed walkers. Clay miners have to know where to step; it's so easy to lose a boot as the suction of the clay is beyond that of ordinary mud. Even in a bright yellow Land Rover drivers have to take care when working around the massive dumpers and bulldozers!

As the water starts to trickle down towards the bottom it has to be guided to the right place. Fresh water from springs or overflow from rains has also to be taken into account in the pumping operations; only clay bearing water is allowed to get right to the bottom. At various points there are pumps to provide high pressure water and to move clay about to different areas. The pit has huge white scars, yet there are fields, trees and even some houses down there. The River Fal, on its way down from The Goss Moor passes unseen along the edge of the pit, carefully kept in place by walls and dykes, following its ancient course and oblivious to the fact that the bottom of the adjacent pit is many feet below its bed. As the water finally reaches the lowest part of the pit, a place known as the sink, the heavier and unwanted sand is allowed to accumulate in sand pits where it will be removed by diggers and loaders, mica is removed using machines known as 'Cyclones'. There is quite a skill to working in the sink, the 'pit bottom man' has the responsibility to ensure that there are not too many sand traps which will slow down the flow of clay bearing water and allow it to settle and be lost whilst at the same time ensuring that the sand will not overflow and 'bury up' the drags, pumps and sumps.

There then begins a process of further refining in order to produce the finest grade of clay. The refining process is highly automated and computerised and consists of mineral processing techniques which are designed to remove the smaller sized waste particles, mainly minerals such as very fine quartz, and mica leaving only the required china clay behind. In all over 60 different grades are produced with both chemically and physically engineered properties. Within these pits can be seen examples of very old technology right up to the most modern. Often when new ways of dealing with the clay were invented they would be put in and tried, if something else came along that was better it would be used but the older machinery might remain in operation alongside. Thus within the Fal Valley area of this pit you can find a waterwheel which was last used in 1942, sand pits and bucket wheels as well as the ultra modern dry mining system.

Clay is continually pumped from the pit bottom up to the large tanks where it settles into a thick slurry. When a request is received from the refinery, underground pipe lines are set, valves opened and pumps are started. Pumping, or landing as it is known, the clay may only take an hour or so but frequent monitoring must be made using instruments

FAL VALLEY PITS

Retew village in the Fal Valley with its Knitting Mill, houses and railway line. On the hill above are the soon-to-be-buried pine trees that gave their name to the sand burrow near Fraddon.

CCHS

This photograph from the sixties shows just how much encroachment had taken place. The knitting factory is close to being engulfed by South Remfry pit, the road will soon be cut off as a through route, but South Fraddon dry next to the railway continued in production.

CCHS

and pressure gauges in order to avoid the disaster of a blown line and subsequent pollution of the watercourses. Once landed at the refiner, the raw clay can undergo a whole series of different processes before being blended into a final grade. For the next step in the process, that is drying, further pumping is required. Clay may travel to Treviscoe or the calciner at Parkandillack before it is dried and either shipped out in bulk or bagged.

This is a very simplified version of what actually goes on, but for the purposes of looking down into the pit from above, the large circular settling tanks to the right at Wheal Remfry can be seen, then up on the skyline is the modern plant at Treviscoe where the final processing may take place. In the valley bottom is an old dry, now disused, but clearly showing how the long low building with a furnace at one end and the chimney at the other was used. The disused Retew branch line runs between the dry and the river. Further down the valley and out of sight beyond the smaller plateau of reclaimed land is the latest and most awesome piece of machinery in the valley.

CORNWALL'S CHINA CLAY COUNTRY

The last load of clay to leave Collins Rotary in the Fal Valley. The lorry, ACV 992 B is an Albion. CCHS

(F) The Dry Mining Plant or 'Dry Miner' as it is often referred to is a five storey block, part building, part machine, and seemingly part dragon. Its working principle is, like so much here, very simple and brings together many of the older techniques into just one building. Around 40% of clay today is obtained using this technique which has been introduced largely to reduce high energy costs associated with the many stages of wet mining. To begin, powerful rubber tyred loading shovels excavate the clay from the quarry face. The broken up rock is taken to a stockpile by slow moving 65 tonne dumpers that require a full flight of steps to get into the cab. From there it is pushed into the top of the Dry Miner using a vast yellow Komatsu loader.

Massive granite boulders are dropped down into the monstrous jaws of the crushers, and as they sink down through the machine the rocks are slowly reduced in size. Material of a size less than 28mm goes into a large washing barrel where a slurry of china clay, sand, mica and gravel is produced. Further classifiers and cyclones produce a product which is mainly china clay whilst the slightly larger materials which spew out from the bottom on conveyor belts are neatly piled up ready to be taken away to be used in the construction industry. To a layman the impression given is that within the bowels of the dragon, and by force of electricity, water and perhaps alchemy a constant slurry of high grade china clay emerges triumphantly ready to be piped away to Melbur refining plant and beyond.

To enter the Dry Miner is a daunting experience. Only a couple of people operate it from a Portakabin using remote control systems, cameras, computers and flashing lights. Even so there are times when the laying on of hands still has to happen. If a boulder is too big to go down through the jaws of the crusher, the operator has to don his ear defenders and hard hat and climb a series of metallic caged stairs. A remote control, similar to the devices used to fly model aircraft is produced to invoke the use of a many jointed mechanical arm with a hammer on it. This will make short work of reluctant boulders. Meanwhile the process can stall, and it is vital to get the thing working full time again. The noise of the crushers, the whine of the motors, the rush of water and the vibration throughout the whole structure somehow combine to make it feel like a living beast. The Dry Miner needs constant feeding and attention, it responds to good handling and it can be extremely expensive if something breaks. But it does the job quicker, cheaper and more efficiently than the more traditional 'wet' method of extraction.

The men and women working here are on the go twenty-four hours a day. This has always been a tradition in the industry. Once there were three shifts per day, forenoons starting at five in the morning, afternoons starting at one and nights starting at nine. Now it's

CORNWALL'S CHINA CLAY COUNTRY

Jack Bunt stopped for his crib at Wheal Remfry.
CCHS

FAL VALLEY PITS

often a more intensive twelve hour shifts, but allowing for longer periods away from work. If you are stuck in a remote monitor cabin or manning a pumping station then the long hours, especially through the night, can be a challenge. You really don't need too many worries that might make you brood.

The man in charge of the pit is always known as the Captain, an ancient term and a mark of respect. In this area to call someone Captain is to confer respectability on them, akin to saying Boss. The industry has of course produced all kinds of slang and technical words and has a vocabulary all of its own. Combine this with a real Cornish dialect and conversations which take place are barely understandable to outsiders. An easy example might be that food is eaten in the Crib Hut, crib being a pasty, sandwiches or in these days possibly a salad. Crib is another word unique to mid Cornwall; in the western part of the county the word Croust is used instead for the same meaning. 'Stankin' roun', balin' the launders with me biddix cos I lost me 'ammer an feelin' brave'n wisht, you!' is slightly more obscure.

To continue with the walk it is possible to return to the top of the zig zag path by going across the middle of the plateau beside the radio mast and back to the car that way. A little shorter but steeper and slippery way is to go through the gate above the mobile home park and follow the path around until its obvious that a worn slope leads directly back down to the kissing gate. Watch it going down here, if in doubt go the long way round!

Meledor Mill on the Retew Branch. Prairie Tank 2-6-2T 5519 leaving with a short train. The empty wagons at the rear are standing at the wharf awaiting loading.
CCHS
H Davies/P Rundle Collection

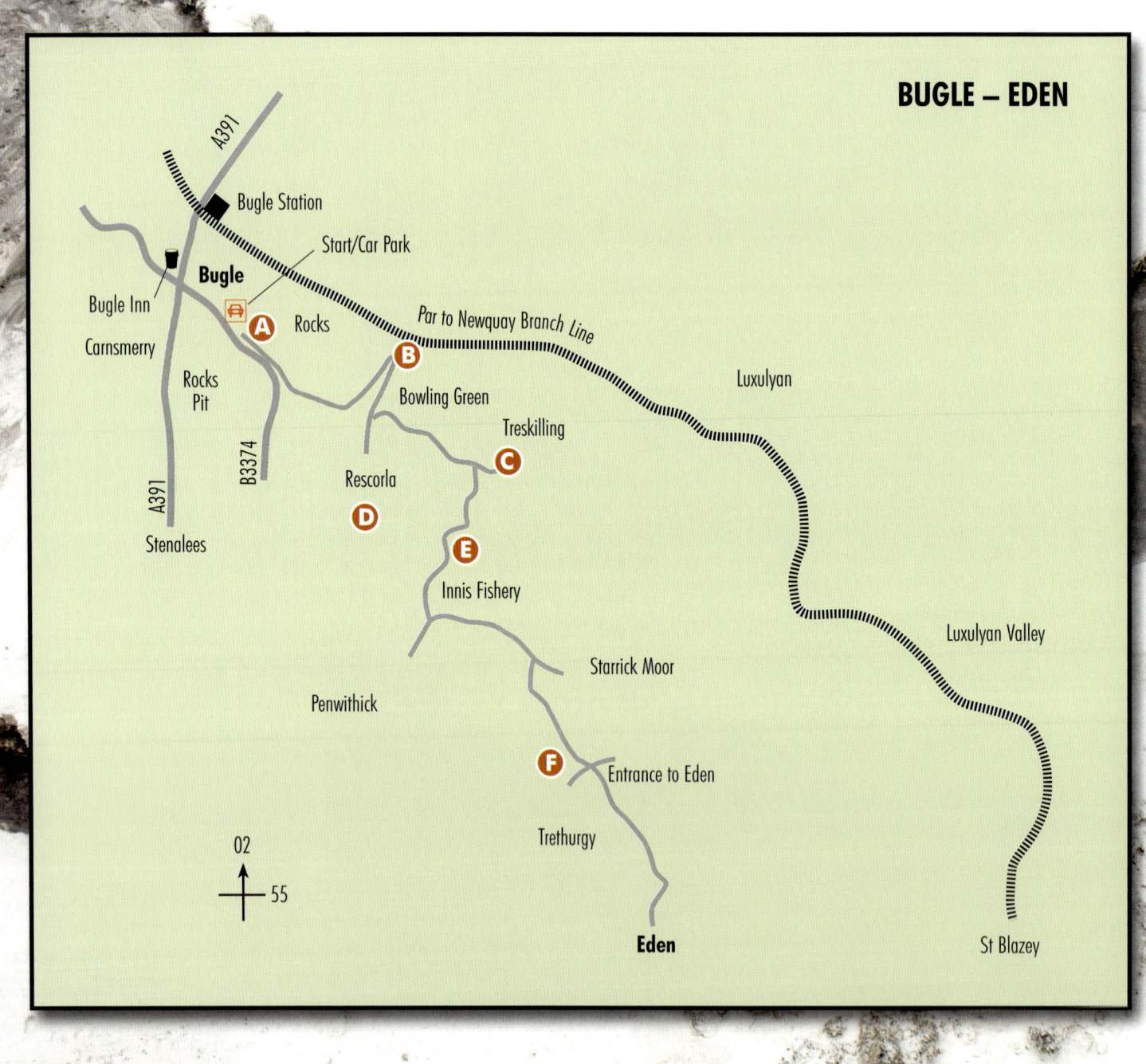

BUGLE TO EDEN

IT IS ABOUT 3 ½ MILES to walk or cycle the signposted clay trail between Bugle and the Eden Project. For about half its length the path is off road, the rest uses public highways shared with cars and other traffic so it is not as free and easy as perhaps some of the others trails in this series. Although here are no toilets or refreshments close to it, Eden provides all the creature comforts when you eventually get to it. Its also fine for off road style pushchairs all the way. There are car parks at both ends and access points all along, so it is quite possible to start in the middle or do sections of the trail at will. Bus services go both to Eden and Bugle from St Austell.

Bugle owes its very existence to the newly emerged Victorian clay mining industry. Before about 1800 there was no village there at all, instead a small group of farms and houses clustered around the sides of the hill and along the edges of the marshy ground. Tin streaming was more evident than clay extraction, the tips which were created as a result of these activities were kept strictly to areas of waste ground or moorland, not being allowed to overspill on to the fields and pastures. Soon though, the potential to make money from the clay deposits began to be understood. Land owners, miners and local farmers saw the need for help as they struggled to get the raw material which they had dug from their own fields and hills, out to the ports and harbours for onward shipment. The roads were few and far between and were poorly constructed. The original main road between Bodmin and St Austell for instance came nowhere near the present village of Bugle, instead it followed the Luxulyan road from Reperry Fork, then branched off through Rescorla and down into the low lying areas around Starrick Moor, eventually meeting the Par roads not far from where The Eden Project is located.

In 1836 a new Turnpike Road was constructed between Bodmin and St Austell that scythed through all the older tracks and fields. It went almost directly up over Hensbarrow, via the gap or pass at Stenalees, then on down the valley and straight into the heart of St Austell. This together with the construction by Joseph Treffry of a tram line, (the one that eventually turned into the railway line from Par and which had its terminus close to the present day

CORNWALL'S CHINA CLAY COUNTRY

124

Bugle Station, transferring clay from horse-drawn wagons on to rail. The casks or barrels were also used to carry clay.

CCHS

A 1910 view of Bugle taken from Goonbarrow showing the Carbean branch line that went up through Stenalees to the mines at Gunheath. At this time the village was only about sixty years old!

C Edyvean

Bugle Station) brought about a revolution in the way that goods were transported. It also created settlements that spread out and along the new transport highway.

An extract from the *West Briton* newspaper of the 7 August 1840 reads thus. 'P. Pinch begs respectfully to announce to the public, the opening of the newly built Bugle Inn at Carnrosemary, which he has fitted up with the utmost attention to neatness and comfort, and he trusts he shall give satisfaction to those who may be pleased to favour him with their support. The House is situated in the midst of the Porcelain Clay Works, about midway between St Austell and Bodmin, on the new line of the road, and is passed daily by the Quicksilver Mail and Regulator Coach. Good stabling and a lock up coach house.' Apparently the inn was named in appreciation of the guard of the Regulator, who had a considerable repertoire of melodies with which he favoured the tin streamers and clay workers as the coach sped over the moors.

The Bugle Inn was used by brokers and dealers to buy and sell minerals, whilst coach and wagon horses were stabled and changed ready for the long haul up and over the hills into St Austell. Around the crossroads by the inn, groups of houses and businesses that

Opposite: *Although not on this route, this dramatic photograph of a derelict water wheel is typical of the many reminders of the industrial past to be found in Clay Country.*

Adrian Brown

125

The installation of temporary rails was a job that was done in the depths of the pits and also in more open countryside. The lines were not of the highest engineering standard, they did not need to be as the wagons were pushed along by hand or pulled by horse. If they came off the track then it was a simple task just to lift them back on again.

C Edyvean

supported the clay mining in the area were created, and from this nucleus the modern village was created.

(A) The start of the trail at Bugle is in a small car park by Rocks Tip on the B3374 Rosevear Road (which is the Bugle to Penwithick road), near the works entrance at Rocks. It is marked by a sculpture in granite of a horse which points in the right direction; all that is to be done is to follow the waymarked track around the edge of the tip. The mature trees here indicate that this sand burrow has been colonised for a long time, although there are plenty of rabbits around that find any newly planted saplings quite appetising. Look out for smaller creatures, wolf spiders that hunt by stealth on the bare sand and digger wasps that nest in the ground stocking their larders with paralysed insects before laying their eggs. After a short while the trail emerges on to the road and turns right.

(B) If one were to turn left away from the marked route and walk a hundred yards or so, the road crosses a railway bridge. This is the line that was built in 1849 by Treffry to serve his newly opened granite and china clay quarries on the eastern edge of the district by connecting the South Coast port of Par with Bugle and ultimately Newquay on the North Coast. Fowey became part of the railway network in 1869. At the point where the road bridge crosses the railway the old goods and passenger trains, whose modern counterparts still use the line to this day, would have struggled up the tortuous climb through the Luxulyan Valley. The footplate crew would have been looking at an easier time for the onward journey, perhaps to pick up a load of clay from Rocks sidings just a short distance further on, or to go to Bugle and the Carbean Branch or even Fraddon Junction with its spur down to Melbur. The fully laden train might have returned to St Blazey on the loop back through St Austell via Parkandillack, but there could equally have been carriage loads of eager passengers en route for the resort town of Newquay, which itself was mainly created by the arrival of the railway. The history of this branch line is fascinating; Treffry built canals, viaducts, tunnels, waterwheels and inclines. His activities are inextricably linked to the early development of the clay industry and its infrastructure, further reading matter on the subject is heartily recommended.

Back to the trail and after emerging on to the public road from the first part of the track, turn right and walk through Bowling Green Village, then left towards Luxulyan still heading for Eden. The road here crosses low marshy ground that in older days would not have been easy to traverse other than by foot. Loaded wagons would have struggled to make much progress as their wheels became bogged down. No matter how hard the horses were driven, the combination of hooves and iron tyres would have made slow

The very first Cornish Unit houses were built at Carnsmerry in Bugle. They are still standing.
CCHS

headway in the deep mud and potholes of those ancient highways. The roads of 200 years ago when the clay industry was just beginning to get into its stride were not built for heavy wheeled traffic. Pack horse trains would have coped easily, sure-footed animals could pick their way from one dry bit of land to another, but it was clear that the new railways and turnpike roads that were being constructed were absolutely necessary if there were to be a continuing expansion of the mining industries. Along this stretch of road there is evidence of present-day land draining with ditches and culverts having been recently constructed. The old way would have tried to pick a delicate path that was high enough to keep out of the marshy areas yet still close enough to the river to make the road as level as possible. As soon as the road comes up out of the valley it is apparent how much better the way underfoot becomes, although by contrast, extra horses would have been required to pull the loads up the gradients.

(C) After a short steep hill the marked clay trail turns right through a gate and down across Treskilling Downs. The view from the gate across the fields and marshes shows just

CORNWALL'S CHINA CLAY COUNTRY

The tiny village of Recorla, like all the other villages, had its own feast week. Centred around the Chapel and Sunday School there were services, games, singing and general celebrations. It was here that the traditional snail dance was performed by the villagers. It has recently been recreated and can be seen during the summer months in the village during their Festival.
C Edyvean

how high the modern tips can be, and it gives a glimpse of the little village of Rescorla just across the valley. Look backwards and it's obvious that the easy way follows the course of the river; the stream here actually is a tributary of the Luxulyan River. For many years there stood beside this road a small steam engine and its attendant winding gear which was built to serve Treskilling Sky Tip. The boiler had suffered, its shed long since fallen to bits, but it was rescued and can now be seen at Morwellham Quay on the banks of the Tamar. The tip no longer exists, having been flattened and re landscaped back into the downs over which you pass. The site where it has been bulldozed shows clearly the invasion, with a help from man, of pioneer plants such as gorse, heather and buddleia all colonising the acidic soils and improving the ground for the future.

(D) Rescorla, almost uniquely amongst villages in the district, has at the present time little modern extra housing development and shows what the small communities were once like. Grouped around the chapel, school and playing field with attendant small meadows and tracks that led to the claypits all around, this village pre dated the clay industry and was an agricultural settlement from much earlier times. Now Rescorla Methodist Chapel is closed for its original purposes, but has been converted into a community resource with

BUGLE TO EDEN

Higher Ninestones pit and engine house. It can be seen how vulnerable the engine houses were to any expansion of the pit, and why so few of them survive to the present.
CCHS

A B117D scrape with a Michigan 280 pusher belonging to 'Western Ex'. The sheer brute power of such machines was necessary to shift the large amounts of overburden around the pits and tips.
CCHS

CORNWALL'S CHINA CLAY COUNTRY

Above left: Goonbarrow near Bugle had a large area devoted to refining the clay. Here in 1910 are mica drags, settling tanks and kilns. The branch line to Newquay and its loop up to Gunheath are visible in the distance. Note that the field boundaries are still preserved at this time and that the village of Bugle is still very small and grouped around the central pub. The fields to the right of the picture would soon be dug up and get lost in the massive Rocks Pit complex.

C Edyvean

Above right: This is probably a general view of Rocks Pit very close to the centre of Bugle village taken in the thirties.

C Edyvean

help from lottery funding and input from Dr Garry Tregidga of the Institute of Cornish Studies. It has at its heart, a determination to promote and celebrate the study of Cornish Culture. Here there is an archive, a computer data base and a meeting place where like minded people can gather together to develop projects concerned with Cornwall's history, literature and performing arts. Rescorla is also the home of the Snail Creep, a Cornish processional dance that has recently been revived after an absence of 60 years and which can be seen being performed at the Annual Rescorla Festival held during May and June.

Continuing with the walk, the track descends through gorse and heathland and goes back to the marshy ground where it winds between pungent, almost stagnant pools that are hidden beneath a covering of rhododendron, rowans, hollies, alders and oaks. Here, hidden from view, are colonies of common frogs, toads and palmate newts, whilst the lichens which grow on the trees and hang from branches harbour many small insects and caterpillars which provide a source of food for chiffchaffs, nuthatches and other insect-eating birds.

(E) Gates and stiles lead to the left and right which go off into other parts of the former Treskilling clay works and disused mica dams and which provide an alternative route, but soon the main track opens up into a fenced off area, a cliff face that has been created in the sands of an old tip. In the sides of the cliff can be seen small holes which are the communal nesting sites of sand martins. There are only two or three hundred breeding pairs in Cornwall, and the clay district is a particularly important place for them. The birds stay around here during the summer but then migrate to tropical West Africa to overwinter. A small shelter allows bird watchers to observe the comings and goings of Treskilling Pit which was last mined in 1971. It has been allowed to flood, and besides becoming a place where local anglers can fish to their hearts content it is the home to many species of wildfowl and other birds. Here can be seen widgeon, teal, snipe, potchard and golden eye. Geese come to feed and seagulls to rest.

The well signed clay trail continues and soon comes out on to the road from Penwithick to Luxulyan. The commercial use of redundant tips and pits has allowed Innis Fishery, to be turned into a restaurant and trout farm as evidenced here. The flooded pits provide excellent fishing, and landscaped mica dams form a backdrop to the ponds. Turn left down the road, watch for the traffic. Soon, opposite a fenced off road, the track turns right; this can be a little difficult to see and might be missed. Uphill through the fields the rocky path runs parallel with the main road to Eden until it meets its main entrance. (F) That's the whole of the trail from Bugle, but of course it is then very easy to link up to the other trails if you are so minded and walk across to Wheal Martyn or into St Austell itself.

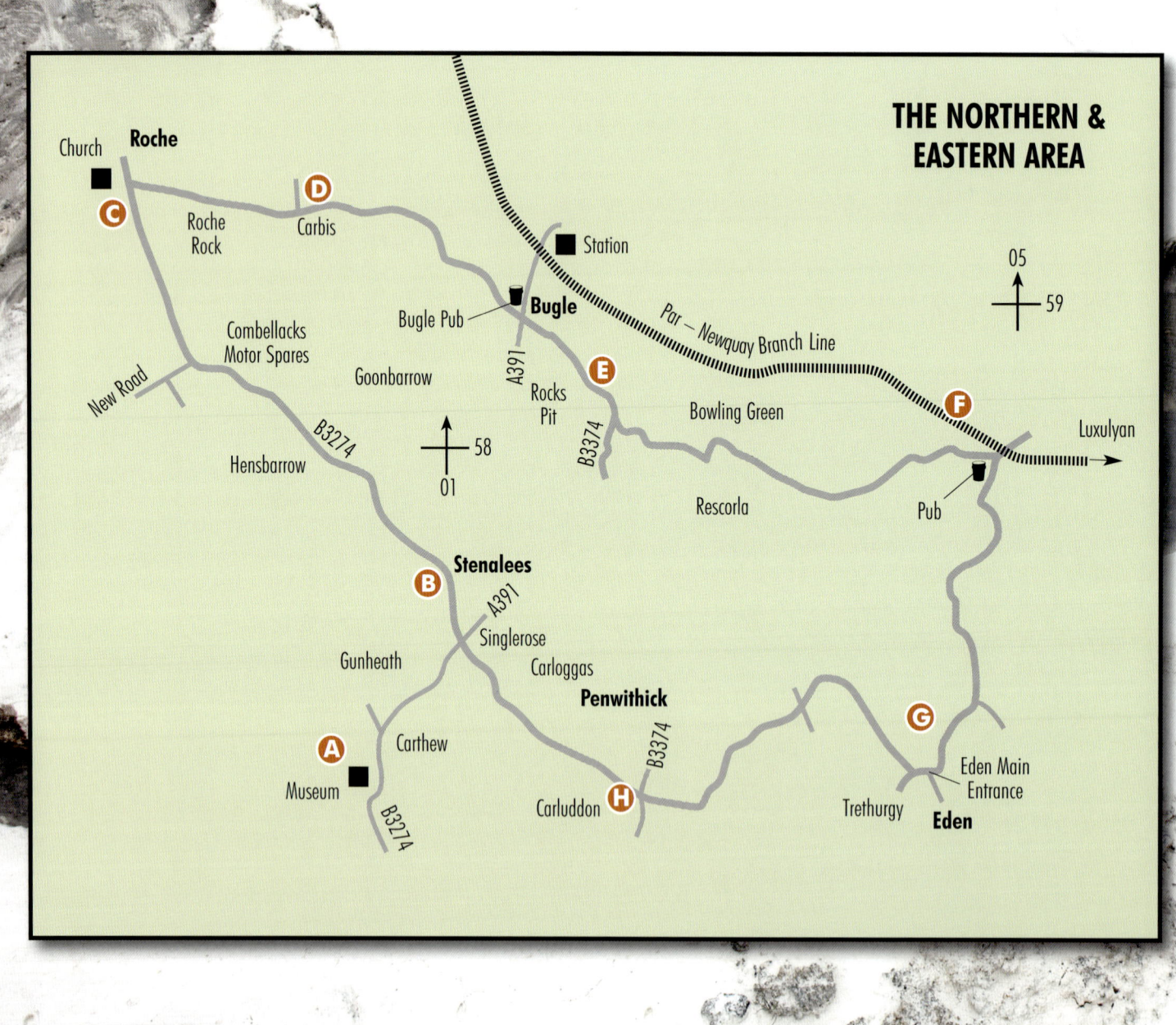

DRIVE 2 – THE NORTHERN AND EASTERN AREA

THIS TEN MILE DRIVE is designed to take in parts of the northern and eastern areas of the china clay district. It is around ten miles long and covers the areas of Stenalees, Roche, Bugle, Luxulyan and Penwithick. Like the previous drive this starts and finishes at the China Clay Country Park on the main St Austell to Bodmin road.

(A) Leave the car park and turn left. At the village of Carthew keep on the main B3274 which passes between the disused pits of Carbean on the left and Lower Ninestones on the right. The railway which was built from Bugle Station to Gunheath Pit crossed the road here and the stone piers of the bridge can be made out where a bridge carrying clay pipe lines, or landing lines as they are known, traverses the highway. Not far from here at the crossroads a tunnel was constructed to take the trains beneath the highest point of the hill at Singlerose and on down into the Stenalees Valley. Most of the rail traffic coming uphill from Bugle would have been empty wagons, the way back down is pretty steep

George Giles and his three-horse team on Singlerose road at Carbean near the present day China Clay Museum.

CCHS

Goonbarrow. Adrian Brown

and good brakes would have been essential as the heavily loaded wagons tried to obey gravity and gain speed on the incline. The line itself was taken up in the late 1960s.

At the small roundabout which marks the place where the newly constructed nineteenth century Turnpike Road crossed the saddle of hills between St Austell and Bodmin turn left towards Roche and Whitemoor on the B3274. Just visible on the grass next to the roundabout is an old monitor, painted red, used to blast the clay from the rocks with high pressure water.

(Straight across the roundabout the road goes down through Stenalees village, following a straight line towards Bugle. The Turnpike itself would have followed the valley bottom to the right down through Treverbyn, but its original course has long since disappeared in the depths of Rocks Pit).

(B) The road to Roche continues to climb, through older established settlements. Close to this place various strands in the development of the area can be seen. The clay industry did not reach this part of the village until the early part of the twentieth century and here and there can be seen the remains of medieval hamlets and farms at Caudledown. There has been much movement of overburden here, mostly from Gunheath, and the old Bluebarrow pit on the left has been filled in and replanted.

The B3274 levels off and then begins to descend. Unfortunately there are few opportunities here to stop and gaze, but the few glimpses of the distant lands beyond the hedges show Bodmin Moor and the countryside up towards Plymouth. In front, along the

Below left: *Goonbarrow Pit with extensive views across to Bodmin Moor and Brown Willy and Rough Tor. Roche is to the left of the picture, Stenalees to the right and beyond and below is Bugle.*
C Edyvean

Below right: *This distant view from Caudledown of the road between Bugle and Stenalees also shows the steep gradient of the Carbean branch line as it makes its way up and over the crest of the hill at Singlerose. Goonbarrow works are in the background.*
C Edyvean

In 1927 a gentleman by the name of Mr Marsden bet that he could push a wheelbarrow loaded with three hundredweight of cement up the hill in Roche. He won!
C Edyvean

line of the road, the Atlantic Ocean gleams in the sunlit distance, and the surfing town of Newquay can be made out. To the left there has been massive land reclamation works, the older craggy terraced landscape has been smoothed off and replanted with heathland and trees. You can pull in here and walk up over for a better view. Although this is well intentioned something of the wild quality, indeed the historical importance of this industrial setting gets lost in the process. Hopefully enough of the untouched scarred and overgrown countryside will be retained to contrast with the all-enveloping reclassification of the land.

Continue on along the road, with the white overgrown peaks of Goonbarrow on the right and drive into the village of Roche. (Just below Goonbarrow, another of the Eco Town developments is planned).

(C) The Norman church here was built around AD1100, and the tower was constructed around the year 1400. Roche is situated half way between china clay country and the Goss Moor, the low lying marshy area that was such a major obstacle to any travellers who may have wished to cross central Cornwall before the railway and the modern roads were built. This is the place where the River Fal rises, but within a few miles are the headwaters of rivers which flow towards Par on the south coast and to the River Camel which enters the sea on the north coast. The villagers of Roche were as used to mining for tin, iron and anything else of value that they could find as they were for clay. They excavated in stone quarries, they farmed the land and did whatever they could to make a living. Outside the church and between two pubs there is a short steep hill. One day in 1927 a man by the name of Marsden from the nearby village of St Dennis made a bet that he could push a wheelbarrow loaded with three hundredweight of cement up the hill. A photograph exists which shows him, surrounded by crowds of people urging him on, or shouting him down, depending on the nature of their bet, as he waits at the bottom with his wooden wheelbarrow. He succeeded in his task and thereafter became a legend, not just in the village but throughout the whole district.

Turn right at the roundabout outside the church and take the road which passes the school and some new houses until it just starts to go down the hill. It is worth stopping here just to look at Roche Rock on the right. Roche Rock is an igneous upthrust of tourmalinised granite dating back millions of years. The ruined chapel on its summit was built in the 15th century and incorporates the base rock as part of its structure and the walls are made of stones quarried from the moors around. No one really knows why it was built, perhaps it was a light or beacon for travellers, or it could have been an imitation of St Michael's

DRIVE 2 – THE NORTHERN AND EASTERN AREA

North Goonbarrow Sand and Stone Depot in about 1936. The mechanism at the top of the burrow allows the skip to automatically tip before returning down the incline to the pit bottom. Beyond is the village of Roche.
CCHS

The Goonbarrow China Clay Mine around 1900.
C Edyvean

An early photograph of North Goonbarrow with stacks of concrete blocks which have been manufactured there. Beyond is the village of Roche.
CCHS

137

DRIVE 2 – THE NORTHERN
AND EASTERN AREA

Littlejohns China Clay Works.
Adrian Brown

CORNWALL'S CHINA CLAY COUNTRY

Miners and farmers were sometimes uneasy neighbours, here a Marshall traction engine works a thrashing machine at Roche, right on the edge of Clay Country.

C Edyvean

A Daimler Milnes bus struggles up the hill past Stenalees Post Office on its way from Bugle to St Austell not long after the First World War.

CCHS

Mount. The legend of Tristan and Iseult is just one of the stories associated with the place, but tradition has it that a hermit lived there and was brought water by his daughter from a hole in the nearby rocks known as Gonettas Well. The Rock stands in a small area of heathland with open access, the footpath can be rocky and the climb to the top difficult, but it is nevertheless well worth a visit simply for the views alone. It is possible to walk across country from here to Tresayes Quarry on the skyline.

Continuing on down the hill the terraced sand burrows and spoil heaps of Goonbarrow are on the right and below, in the valleys, are the remains of tin streaming works which predate the china clay mines. If you look carefully you can also make out the medieval field patterns, the small stone-hedged fields which still exist in the margins of the landscape. **(E)** Next to the road on the right are some newly-converted holiday homes at Carbis Wharf. The two long buildings were clay dries and were reached by a short branch line from Bugle that crossed the road just below the site. The curious upturned bottle-shaped building in the centre, along with the chimney stacks was once a works that produced bricks for clay dry furnaces and housing. You may still come across piles of bricks with their makers' names on; Carbis also produced them for general building

DRIVE 2 – THE NORTHERN AND EASTERN AREA

purposes. Continue on down the valley and the first houses in Bugle begin to appear. The origins of the name and the foundations of the village have already been discussed, but it is easy to appreciate how the pub was at the beginning of the present-day settlement. Just before the crossroads there is a disused railway bridge that carried the Carbean line which looped around and above the village forming the lower end of the track to Stenalees and incorporating the sidings at Goonbarrow before eventually going on up to Gunheath.

Go across the crossroads by the traffic lights in the centre of the village and drive towards Penwithick on the B3374. **(F)** Pass the car park with the granite horse on the left that is the start of the clay trail to Eden, then turn left off the main road towards Bowling Green and continue to the junction. Turn left then almost immediately right towards Luxulyan. That lovely Victorian railway carriage which has been turned into a house was once one of many such adaptations for those who could not afford blocks and mortar. Redundant carriages, wagons and trucks found all kinds of uses but these have now been superseded by second-hand containers or boxes from lorries which perhaps do not have the same kind of aesthetic appeal as the earlier conversions. At this point the route uses the same ground as the Bugle to Eden trail, however when that trail turns right and goes through

This is Carbis and the railway wagons are being loaded with casked clay. They will be taken down to Bugle station, about half a mile away for onward shipment.
CCHS

Grass track racing near Treviscoe just after the war. Local ace Adrian Kessell cut his competitive teeth at such events, he was still racing and winning when he was well into his seventies.

CORNWALL'S CHINA CLAY COUNTRY

the gate at Treskilling Down, drivers need to carry on up the hill and through the hamlet of Treskilling. The road crosses, or more correctly bridges, some low ground after which it emerges close to the station and pub in Luxulyan.

(G) Luxulyan is probably best known for its nearby valley, a site of tremendous industrial and archeological importance. Its steeply wooded valley contains many early industrial remains including the viaduct built by Treffry, and was designated a World Heritage Site in 2006. The railway through the valley still carries trains with up to 1140 tonnes of china clay down to Par and on to the docks at Fowey. The Luxulyan Valley is well worth a visit, but is not included in this route as it is rather off course and needs much more attention than just this chapter can give.

Turn right by the pub. This road follows the much older route to the coast from the inland mining areas. The longer but flatter way to the ports circumnavigated the hills and dropped down into the coastal region through St Blazey, Bodelva and Tregrehan. In a couple of miles the road passes the main entrance to The Eden Project where there is a roundabout.

(H) Turn right here, this stretch was recently constructed to cope with the traffic that goes to Eden and passes Trebal Refinery which is the largest of the three clay refineries and deals with five hundred thousand tonnes of clay per annum. The village of Penwithick is on the right whilst to the left is Baal Pit where there is a proposal to start the first of the Eco Towns. At the mini roundabout go across, and follow the signs back towards the

Below left: *This photograph of Carthew Clay Works at Gunheath was taken in 1927. It shows the inclined track of the sky tip with, part way up, a laden skip on its way to the top. The internal railway system that brought stent to be loaded into the skip can also be seen.*

C Edyvean

Below right: *A good general view of Carthew Clay works showing the engine house, the inclined track for the skip, a sky tip, settling tanks, micas and much of the other launders, pipes and other paraphernalia which made up the works in 1927.*

C Edyvean

Mica Stream.

Adrian Brown

China Clay Country Park. **(I)** On the left is the old pyramid sky tip that will be left as a monument to the clay industries past and which also acts as a navigational aid for sailors way out in St Austell Bay. The defunct mica dams at Carluddon are another Eco Town site. On the right are the replanted slopes of Carloggas Downs whilst the reclaimed areas of Penhale overlook the valleys that lead to Bugle on the right or St Austell on the left. Now the route is back at the crossroads at Stenalees, close to the start of this drive. Turn left and after a mile or so the museum appears on the right. Have a cup of tea, the cakes are very good!

BIBLIOGRAPHY

Thurlow, Charles. *China Clay*, Tor Mark, 1992

Thurlow, Charles. *China Clay from Devon and Cornwall*, Cornish Hillside Publications 2006

Thurlow, Charles and Perry, Ronald. *An extraordinary Earth, (China Clay, China Stone, Ball Clay, Soapstone from Cornwall, Devon and Dorset 1700-1914)*, Cornish Hillside Publications 2010

Cornish Steam Preservation Society, *Pit to Port*, 2009

Barton, R.M. *Life in Cornwall in the Mid Nineteenth Century*, Bradford Barton 1971

Turner, Mike. *Clay Country Voices*, Tempus, 2000

Larn, Bridget and Richard. *Charlestown*, Tor Mark 2006

Body, Geoffrey. *Cornwall Railway*, Avon Anglia, 1984

Williams, Michael. *My Cornwall*, Bossinney Books, 1973

St Stephen in Brannel Parish Council. *A Century of Change*, 1994

Wheal Martyn China Clay Museum. *Guide*

Imerys Clay Country Vision, pamphlet, 2003

Kellys Directory of Cornwall 19th to mid 20th century.

Hudson, Kenneth. *A History of English China Clays* (50th anniversary), David and Charles 1969

Burton R M. *A History of the Cornish Clay Industry*, D B Barton, 1969

Dart, Maurice. *Mineral Railways of East Cornwall*, Middleton Press 2004